*Nikola Tesla, page 17*

# TIME
## SECRETS OF
# GENIUS

Discovering the nature of brilliance

# TIME

MANAGING EDITOR  Richard Stengel
DESIGN DIRECTOR  D.W. Pine
DIRECTOR OF PHOTOGRAPHY  Kira Pollack

# SECRETS OF GENIUS
Discovering the nature of brilliance

EDITOR  Neil Fine
DESIGNER  Anne-Michelle Gallero
PHOTO EDITOR  Patricia Cadley
CONSULTING EDITOR  Skye Gurney
WRITERS  Gary Belsky, David Bjerklie, John Cloud, Geoff Colvin,
Sean Gregory, Lev Grossman, Jeffrey Kluger, Kelly Knauer,
Michael Lemonick, Harry McCracken, Regina Nuzzo, James Poniewozik,
Ellen Shapiro, Joel Stein, Maia Szalavitz
REPORTERS  Lena Finkel, Damien Scott, Jenisha Watts
COPY EDITOR  Kathleen A. Kelly
EDITORIAL PRODUCTION  David Sloan

TIME HOME ENTERTAINMENT
PUBLISHER  Jim Childs
VICE PRESIDENT, BRAND AND DIGITAL STRATEGY  Steven Sandonato
EXECUTIVE DIRECTOR, MARKETING SERVICES  Carol Pittard
EXECUTIVE DIRECTOR, RETAIL AND SPECIAL SALES  Tom Mifsud
EXECUTIVE PUBLISHING DIRECTOR  Joy Butts
DIRECTOR, BOOKAZINE DEVELOPMENT AND MARKETING  Laura Adam
FINANCE DIRECTOR  Glenn Buonocore
ASSOCIATE PUBLISHING DIRECTOR  Megan Pearlman
ASSISTANT GENERAL COUNSEL  Helen Wan
ASSISTANT DIRECTOR, SPECIAL SALES  Ilene Schreider
BRAND MANAGER  Bryan Christian
ASSOCIATE PREPRESS MANAGER  Alex Voznesenskiy
ASSOCIATE BRAND MANAGER  Isata Yansaneh
ASSOCIATE BOOK PRODUCTION MANAGER  Kimberly Marshall

EDITORIAL DIRECTOR  Stephen Koepp
COPY CHIEF  Rina Bander
DESIGN MANAGER  Anne-Michelle Gallero

SPECIAL THANKS TO: Katherine Barnet, Jeremy Biloon, Susan Chodakiewicz,
Rose Cirrincione, Jacqueline Fitzgerald, Christine Font, Jenna Goldberg,
Hillary Hirsch, David Kahn, Amy Mangus, Nina Mistry, Dave Rozzelle,
Ricardo Santiago, Adriana Tierno, Vanessa Wu, Time Inc. Premedia

Copyright © 2013 Time Home Entertainment Inc.
Published by TIME Books, an imprint of Time Home Entertainment Inc.
135 West 50th Street • New York, NY 10020

ISBN 10: 1-61893-084-2
ISBN 13: 978-1-61893-084-2
Library of Congress control number: 2013938717

Some articles in this book were previously published in substantially the same form in TIME magazine.

# TABLE OF CONTENTS

GENIUS AT WORK
28

A FIRE IN THE FLINT
By Lev Grossman
6

THE NATURE OF GENIUS
8

INSIDE THE DAZZLING MIND
By John Cloud
10

MIND OVER MADNESS
By Maia Szalavitz
22

SPEAK OF THE DEVIL
By Jeffrey Kluger
26

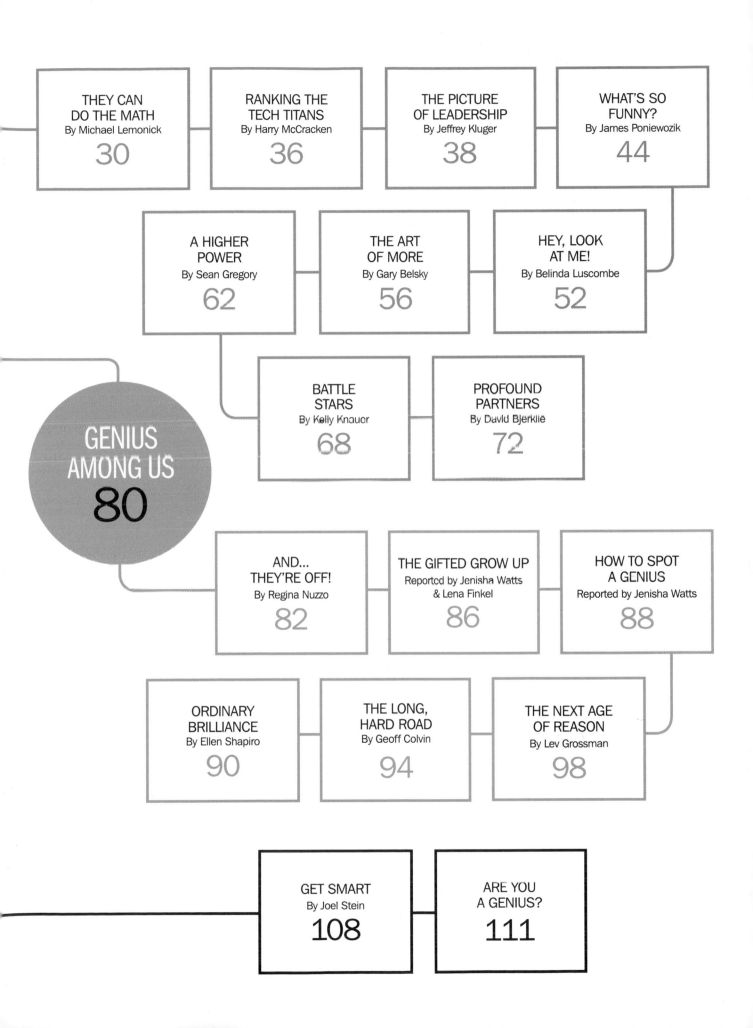

THEY CAN
DO THE MATH
By Michael Lemonick
30

RANKING THE
TECH TITANS
By Harry McCracken
36

THE PICTURE
OF LEADERSHIP
By Jeffrey Kluger
38

WHAT'S SO
FUNNY?
By James Poniewozik
44

A HIGHER
POWER
By Sean Gregory
62

THE ART
OF MORE
By Gary Belsky
56

HEY, LOOK
AT ME!
By Belinda Luscombe
52

GENIUS
AMONG US
80

BATTLE
STARS
By Kelly Knauer
68

PROFOUND
PARTNERS
By David Bjerklie
72

AND...
THEY'RE OFF!
By Regina Nuzzo
82

THE GIFTED GROW UP
Reported by Jenisha Watts
& Lena Finkel
86

HOW TO SPOT
A GENIUS
Reported by Jenisha Watts
88

ORDINARY
BRILLIANCE
By Ellen Shapiro
90

THE LONG,
HARD ROAD
By Geoff Colvin
94

THE NEXT AGE
OF REASON
By Lev Grossman
98

GET SMART
By Joel Stein
108

ARE YOU
A GENIUS?
111

# A FIRE IN THE FLINT

## BY LEV GROSSMAN

*Genius is a difficult idea to grasp, by turns admired and suspect. We have clues to what sparks it, but far more mysteries to solve*

**W**HAT IS A GENIUS? WILLIAM Shakespeare was a genius. Then again, when he was alive, everyone was. In his day the word "genius" meant your personality, the distinctive essence that made you who you are. It didn't necessarily mean that you were brilliant or even particularly clever. It just meant that you were you.

ORVIDAS

The idea of genius is an old one, and its meaning has shifted and transformed in curious ways over the centuries. To the Romans a genius was a spirit that belonged to a person or a place, a kind of ghostly companion who determined one's identity and one's fate. Genius only became something exceptional in the 18th century, when a rather magical idea arose: that there was an entirely other order of human beings, possessed of an ineffable extra mental increment that enabled them to do things we ordinary people couldn't. "Weave a circle round him thrice, / And close your eyes with holy dread," Coleridge wrote in "Kubla Khan." "For he on honey-dew hath fed, / And drunk the milk of Paradise." As democratic revolutions swept Europe and America, deposing nobilities left and right, the cult of genius created a new kind of aristocracy: an aristocracy of the mind.

Not that being a genius was all milk and honey-dew. To be a genius was to be both blessed and cursed, to be both more and less than human. Geniuses were misunderstood and ostracized by society. ("The public is wonderfully tolerant," Oscar Wilde wrote. "It forgives everything except genius.") They had a worrying tendency to die young: the death of English poet John Keats of tuberculosis at 25 was a tragedy, but it also confirmed his greatness. Keats, in turn, admired the poet Thomas Chatterton, who poisoned himself when he was only 17. In fact, the list of actual geniuses who've ended their own lives runs from Diane Arbus to Stefan Zweig.

No surprise there. Genius was long believed to correlate strongly with eccentricity and mental illness—"Great wits are sure to madness near allied," Dryden wrote, "and thin partitions do their bounds divide." Scientists are currently exploring the idea of a genetic link between genius and schizophrenia, and abundant anecdotal evidence supports the hypothesis. According to Plutarch, Archimedes never washed and had to be dragged to the public baths, where he sat doodling geometric figures in the dust with his fingers. Before Nikola Tesla would eat a meal, he required precisely 18 napkins, which he used to obsessively polish his place settings.

But it's not genes or hygiene that separates geniuses from the common run of humanity. It's something else, something wild and unquantifiable that can neither be taught or reverse-engineered. It arrives unannounced and leaves the same way; French poet-prodigy Arthur Rimbaud, for example, gave up writing poetry by the time he was 20. It doesn't run in families; Leonardo da Vinci was the son of a notary and a peasant, and Isaac Newton's father was an illiterate yeoman. It correlates strongly with talent and high intelligence but also differs from them in subtle ways. "Talent hits a target no one else can hit," wrote German philosopher Arthur Schopenhauer. "Genius hits a target no one else can see." Geniuses have always been the best commentators on their own unusual qualities of mind. Said Samuel Johnson: "A genius, whatever it be, is like a fire in the flint, only to be produced by collision with a proper subject."

We live in an age that is both reverent of genius and skeptical of it at the same time. The current trend is to deconstruct it, or at any rate to diffuse and disperse it. Books like Malcolm Gladwell's *Outliers: The Story of Success* and Steven Johnson's *Where Good Ideas Come From* have undermined the myth of the lonely, misunderstood thinker, emphasizing instead the importance of the world around the person: family, education, resources, collaborators. Austrian-born philosopher Ludwig Wittgenstein was unquestionably a clever fellow, but would we know him as a genius if he hadn't been born into one of the richest families in Europe? Historical forces inevitably play a part as well. Sometimes the world seems to spontaneously bring genius into being, to demand it from humanity. Newton and Gottfried Leibniz developed calculus in almost balletic sync with each other, 500 miles apart. Charles Darwin and Alfred Russel Wallace formulated the theory of evolution simultaneously. As Ralph Waldo Emerson wrote: "When Nature has work to be done, she creates a genius to do it."

We might be more comfortable if genius could be explained away, rendered mundane and comprehensible by history or genetics or neurology—or, for that matter, spirits. Genius is simply a difficult idea to accept. Inherently undemocratic, it doesn't sit well with our flat, egalitarian, crowd-sourced worldview. In many ways the Shakespearean age's notion of genius would be more palatable.

Then again, there is always the possibility that we're all potential geniuses, fires in the flint in search of our proper subject, though in most cases destined never to find it. In the pages that follow, we'll probe and measure genius, learning whatever we mere mortals can about what happens when the spark is struck. Of course, genius can't be reduced to a set of rules. In fact, if it has an essence, it is in the breaking of rules. So the nature of genius will remain a great mystery, even as the clues it has left behind are the masterpieces of civilization.

# THE NATURE OF GENIUS

# INSIDE THE DAZZLING MIND

BY JOHN CLOUD

*Science is learning that geniuses may be born that way—but they also need to be nurtured for their true brilliance to emerge*

N NOVEMBER 1929, AN EXTRAORDINARY GIRL WAS BORN IN BANGALORE, INDIA. AS SHAKUNTALA DEVI grew, it became clear that her brain functioned far more efficiently than did other kids'. She could solve equations so rapidly that her father, a sometime circus performer, began to think the girl's talents might gain a popular audience. He was right.

Eventually, Devi would travel the globe calculating—in her head, in a few seconds—answers to such problems as the multiplication of, say, 7,686,369,774,870 by 2,465,099,745,749. At a London demonstration in 1980, Devi was given exactly those digits. She offered the correct product—18,947,668,177,995,426,462,773,730—in fewer than 30 seconds.

Devi performed such feats for decades. For her, arithmetic came as naturally as reciting the days of the week; in fact, given a date in the preceding century, Devi could accurately state the weekday on which it had fallen. She was an intellectual force who was called a genius throughout much of her life, which ended in April 2013 at the age of 83.

Yet she made little lasting contribution. Her *New York Times* obituary was tepid: in her later years, Devi had become an "astrologer, cookbook author, and novelist." The *Times* failed to note that in the 1970s, she had written an intensely thorough history of homosexuality that bolstered what was then a fledgling movement for gay rights. Then again, the book had fallen out of print years earlier. The child genius grew into an admirable but not especially influential adult.

Which raises the question, What is a genius? If it's not someone like Devi, with her vanishingly rare math talent, who qualifies? Well, Albert Einstein, of course. It's difficult even to think of the word without conjuring his name. But Einstein didn't seem particularly exceptional as a boy; he even had trouble speaking. And though that early disability may sometimes be overemphasized—his biographer Walter Isaacson notes that Einstein excelled at the Munich schools he attended—it was only after supplementary education by mentors such as his uncle Jakob, an engineer, that Einstein was able to write his influential scientific papers.

**EVERYTHING IS RELATIVE**
*Sure, Einstein was smart, but would he have grown into a historically important physicist had he not had good mentors and teachers?*

Others whom we have proclaimed to be geniuses seem to have sprung into the world fully formed. Mozart is said to have been composing music by age 5 or 6; by 8, he was writing symphonies and playing flawlessly from sheets of music he had never laid eyes on—"like an adult reading from a text," as Boston College professor Ellen Winner writes in her book *Gifted Children: Myths and Realities*. If Einstein's talents were at least partly cultivated, Mozart's seem almost involuntary. But we call both men geniuses, and that suggests that genius is as much a cultural invention as a measurable aptitude. It can be born or made—or both.

And so we ask again: What exactly is genius?

IN AN OLD AND SIMPLISTIC FORMULATION, THE debate about genius pits nature versus nurture: either geniuses naturally rise to the top, or social institutions help to lift them from the bottom. But in the past decade, new research has complicated our fundamental understanding of intelligence. Brain studies of children and the aged have shown that crucial neural pathways can develop in a year or take as long as a decade to function properly—and they can decay just as capriciously. For example, according to research out of the University of Iowa, playing a video game

for just 10 hours over a few weeks not only can halt the decline of mental processing power among those over 50 but actually increase it.

At the same time, social ideas about genius are changing. People with autism and Asperger's syndrome were previously identified as disabled. Today, their intellectual abilities are being recognized. The animal expert and autism activist Temple Grandin has famously developed more efficient and humane methods of raising and slaughtering animals—methods that have changed modern husbandry. And even as we reconsider the nature of intelligence, a lively debate has begun over what might be called the 10-or-10 rule of genius. As popularized by writer Malcolm Gladwell in his book *Outliers: The Story of Success*, it states that someone can achieve lasting influence in a field—any field, from chemistry to singing to pitching for a baseball team—only after 10 years of dedication or 10,000 hours of practice. That's how long it takes, the argument goes, to earn the right to be called a genius. By these criteria, Nick D'Aloisio wouldn't qualify, though his development, at 15, of the smartphone app Summly and its subsequent sale to Yahoo made him one of the world's youngest self-made millionaires.

A leader in disentangling these knots is psychologist Dean Keith Simonton, who has studied intellectual eminence since his Harvard grad school days in the 1970s. In his 2009 book *Genius 101*, Simonton—a distinguished professor at the University of California, Davis—provides the term with a rigorous if ponderous definition: Geniuses are those who not only "have the intelligence, enthusiasm, and endurance to acquire the needed expertise in a broadly valued domain of achievement" but who also make contributions to that field that can be considered both "original and highly exemplary."

Fully unraveling these threads, though, has to begin with determining if that first attribute—intelligence—can in fact be adequately calculated.

The idea of an intelligence measure has its roots in tests created by Alfred Binet, a French psychologist in the late 1800s who was fascinated by the performance of chess players who could even beat their opponents blindfolded. He invited some of those winners to his offices, and so began the Binet tests.

Binet eventually asked hundreds of young people, the vast majority of them French adolescent males, to complete questionnaires

**CREATURE COMFORTER** *Activist and animal expert Temple Grandin has changed our view of autistic intelligence.*

**YOUNG MONEY** *Nick D'Aloisio developed his first smartphone app at the age of 12. In 2013, the 17-year-old Brit sold his Summly app to Yahoo for a reported $30 million and was hired by the company as a full-time employee.*

and solve equations. He continued to conduct tests for years, but at the time of his death, in 1911, he had not yet developed a satisfactory measure of intelligence. A few years later, researchers at Stanford University helped to refine the Binet test, and the Stanford-Binet scales became the first widely accepted standards for the evaluation of IQ.

Binet started with an idiosyncratic sample: accomplished Parisian boys; although statisticians and sociologists worked subsequently for years to erase signs of bias from the test, the very concept of IQ has always been held under the suspicion that it's really just a way to judge one privileged European kid against another. In the mid-20th century, German eugenicists misused IQ scores and anecdotes of genius to help create the race-based theory that some people from Northern Europe were more likely to show genius than those whose families could be traced to other parts of the world. After the idea of genius became enmeshed with the idiocy of eugenics, it was decades before public educators would again think about offering special services for gifted children or even trying to identify them.

When they did so, most children labeled "gifted" continued to be boys, and even today, female geniuses are often ignored. As recently as 2009, a team led by Margarita Bianco at the University of Colorado, Denver, found that a group of mixed-gender educators assigned to read profiles of Darin and Doreen, a pair of exceptional (and fictional) students, were far more likely to refer Darin to a gifted program, even though the accomplishments of the two candidates were identical. That's a problem for society, because genius emerges so often—as it did in Einstein and Marie Curie, Henri Matisse and Mary Cassatt—only after young talent has been enriched and refined by educators.

Our ideas about how to define genius are clearly colored by preconceptions about gender. Think of 10 people in history whom you'd consider consensus choices as geniuses. How many women are on your list? As the influential feminist Julia Kristeva has pointed out, the term "genius" is already a "provocative hyperbole"—one that often ignores the childhood advantages that many highly accomplished people enjoy. When gender stereotypes are piled on top of that hyperbole, we find ourselves inevitably in an all-male alcove. No one ever really wins the parlor-room argument about whether Picasso or da Vinci was the greater genius, but either way it's a stacked deck: the scientists Marie Curie and her daughter Irene, the political philosopher Hannah Arendt and the artist Frida Kahlo never even get mentioned.

To be fair, that's partly because, historically, many

# A Genius Hall of Fame BY MICHAEL NEILL

### ◀ Marie Curie
#### THE CHEMIST
In 1903, Curie (born Maria Salomea Skłodowska, in Poland) was awarded the Nobel Prize for Physics. Eight years later, she won another, in chemistry. Her mere presence was a reproach to an all-male scientific establishment that tried to block her at every turn, but in the end all her opponents could do was marvel. She discovered and named two elements, polonium and radium. She coined the word "radioactivity" with her husband and collaborator, Pierre Curie. And she pioneered the use of radiation therapy to treat cancer patients. But perhaps most important of all, she forever set an example for every little girl who decides she wants a chemistry set for her next birthday.

exceptionally intelligent women hid their identities or let their achievements be subsumed by their workmate husbands. The Brontë sisters published under male names, and, as Joshua Wolf Shenk notes in his forthcoming book *Powers of Two: The Story of Creative Pairs*, the extraordinary contributions of Ava Miller to the achievements of her husband, Nobel laureate Linus Pauling, are rarely acknowledged.

During the 1970s and '80s, psychometricians—men and women who study how to measure intelligence—worked relentlessly and more or less successfully to rid IQ tests of any meaningful variance based on gender (or race or income). But a new genius-defining question quickly took their place: What made top scorers on standardized tests like the SAT successful? By that point, the debate had become more political than psychometric, and it came to a boil in 1994 when the Free Press published a dense book on psychological data called *The Bell Curve: Intelligence and Class Structure in American Life*. It would probably have been ignored if not for the cultural battle then raging over race, genes and success. The authors—Richard Herrnstein, a well-respected research psychologist who died shortly after the book was released, and Charles Murray, a writer widely admired among conservatives—argued that IQ data showed persistent differences between whites and African Americans. But Herrnstein and Murray wrote little about the cultural and historical context of IQ and genius, virtually ignoring those highly advantaged Parisian chess champions who had helped Binet develop his IQ test in the first place.

IQ WILL ALWAYS BE CONTESTED TERRITORY. BUT then, intelligence doesn't entirely determine whether

## ◀ William Shakespeare

### THE PLAYWRIGHT

Francis Bacon, Edward de Vere, Christopher Marlowe—over the centuries, almost every prominent Elizabethan able to lift a quill pen has been proposed as the author of the 38 plays, 154 sonnets and all the rest of a singularly astonishing oeuvre. One by one, their partisans' claims have been discredited, and when they are, credit comes back around to the unassuming theater manager from Stratford-upon-Avon. In *Macbeth* and *Hamlet*, *King Lear* and *Othello*, the Bard plumbed the soul of power and exposed the rot inside. His sonnets include some of the greatest expressions of love ever composed. In Ben Jonson's words, Shakespeare is "not of an age, but for all time."

## Sun Tzu ▶

### THE WARRIOR

Historians dispute his name, and they differ over what century he graced—maybe the sixth B.C., maybe later, say around the time of Rome's rise. They know nothing about the life he lived or if he ever actually existed at all. One fact, however, is certain: someone in that faraway time was responsible for writing *The Art of War*, and its exhortations, adopted by modern fighters from the U.S. Marines to Mao Zedong, remain as fresh as the day he jotted them down. "A leader leads by example, not force," he wrote. And "There is no instance of a nation benefiting from prolonged warfare." Two millennia before another oft-consulted military theorist, Carl von Clausewitz, Sun Tzu, whoever he was, laid down the real rules for battlefield victory.

a person will be seen as a genius anyway. In his 1790 book *The Critique of Judgment*, philosopher Immanuel Kant defined genius as "a talent for which no definite rule can be given." Genius, he wrote, is "not an aptitude in the way of cleverness"—that is, it is not something you can fake. Kant believed that genius exists only when ideas are both original and exemplary—and that, alas, disqualifies human computers such as Devi (who was born more than a century after Kant's death), no matter how huge the sums they can calculate in their heads.

Once again the debate reveals itself as something of a tautology: genius is the combination of originality and excellence, thoughtfulness lashed to innovation. Compounding the issue is this knotty problem: Who exactly will figure out how to quantify any of those qualities?

Well, Simonton, for one. The University of California professor has tried to determine ways to implement Kant's definition of original and exemplary work. One method he and others have used is to count the number of times an individual's publications are cited in professional literature or the number of times a composer's work is performed and recorded. Other investigators have counted encyclopedia references. Such methods may not be terribly sophisticated, but they at least lead us away from the realm of pure philosophy. Names such as Einstein, Newton, da Vinci and Shakespeare regularly appear in such catalogs. Michelangelo, Picasso and Mozart, too. You might have to look harder, though, to find putative geniuses such as Toni Morrison and Scott Joplin.

All these great men and women seem noncon-

## ◀ Pelé
### THE GOLDEN BOOT

Combine Jordan's otherworldly athleticism with the lethal accuracy of Ali's jab, mix in the sheer joy of a 6-year-old who's just scored his first goal, and you approach the essence of the man the International Olympic Committee designated Athlete of the Century in 1999. Edson Arantes do Nascimento (named for another genius, Thomas Edison) started out kicking a sock stuffed with newspaper and soared into soccer's stratosphere—three World Cups, 1,281 goals and unanimous acclaim as the best player ever. His post-career career as a humanitarian and goodwill ambassador was tarnished in 2013, however, when he urged Brazilians to forgo the protests sweeping the country in favor of rooting for the national team. Even a soccer idol, it seems, can have feet of clay.

## Archimedes ▶
### THE SCIENCE GUY

Living in Syracuse, a major Greek city in Sicily, in the third century B.C., he is remembered today mainly as an inventor and engineer. Make no mistake; he was both. More important, though, he was one of the great mathematicians of all time; it would be 1,200 years or more before the likes of Isaac Newton, Johannes Kepler and Pierre de Fermat caught up with his thinking. He was also the father of what we now call pure science. As Plutarch put it, "He placed his whole affection and ambition in those purer speculations where there can be no reference to the vulgar needs of life."

troversial choices; their creations, purposeful and particular, are their argument. But what to do with accidental genius? Simonton holds up the case of biologist Alexander Fleming, who in 1928 "noticed quite by chance that a culture of *Staphylococcus* had been contaminated by a blue-green mold. Around the mold was a halo." Bingo: penicillin. Fleming is now understood to be one of the great scientists of the 20th century, a man whose work has saved literally millions of lives. And, yes, Fleming did eventually isolate the active substance in what he named *Penicillium notatum*. But all his further groundbreaking work was built on chance. Suppose you had been in Fleming's lab that day and happened to be the one to notice the halo around the mold. Would you be the genius?

Recently, some writers have used "accidental" geniuses such as Fleming to emphasize the hard work

and endurance so often required to achieve original and exemplary accomplishments. One impetus for this shift in emphasis away from brute-force intelligence is the research of Anders Ericsson, who teaches psychology at Florida State University. Ericsson has shown that mastering many complex human endeavors requires a minimum of 10 years' experience. The 10-year rule was posited as long ago as 1899, when *Psychological Review* ran a paper that concluded that it takes at least that long to become expert in the noble pursuit of telegraphy.

But if 10 years is a necessary minimum to achieve expertise in most fields, it is no guarantee of success, let alone genius. As Ericsson concludes in the 901-page *Cambridge Handbook of Expertise and Expert Performance* (2006), "The number of years of experience in a domain is a poor predictor of attained

### ◀ Nikola Tesla
**THE ELECTRIC GENERATOR**

By the end of his life, in 1943, Tesla had become almost a parody of the mad scientist— a germophobic recluse who dismissed Einstein's work, wandered in the vile swamplands of eugenics and told anyone who would listen that he was working on a ray that could destroy 10,000 enemy aircraft. Long before that, however, he had invented, discovered or envisioned, among other wonders, fluorescent light, remote control, the laser and the vertical-takeoff aircraft. And in 1893, thanks to the alternating-current transformers he invented, Tesla lit up the Chicago World's Fair, showing the world just how bright its future would be.

performance." That's partly because experience can result in a psychological problem that is a sometime consequence of extreme intelligence: overconfidence. A 2000 study in the Journal *Accident Analysis & Prevention* found that licensed race-car drivers—the geniuses of the speedway—had significantly more on-the-road accidents than regular drivers. As the work of Ericsson and others has shown, being thought of as a genius—or thinking of yourself as one—can be a fast route to failure. (See page 96 for a full account of Ericsson's work on whether practice makes perfect.)

The *Cambridge Handbook* concludes that great performance comes mostly from many years' practice but also from another activity: regularly obtaining accurate feedback. Like Einstein, many true geniuses don't emerge fully formed; mentors help mulch the overgrown ground of their thoughts and ideas. In a 1997 study published in the journal *Medical Decision Making*, researchers noted that although only 4% of interns had known a group of elderly patients for more than a week, while nearly half the highly experienced attending physicians had known them for more than six months, the attending physicians—with their professional and interpersonal advantages—were no more accurate than the interns at predicting the patients' end-of-life preferences, a crucial factor in achieving a good and peaceful death. It was attention to the patients' feelings and values that mattered, not a more in-depth knowledge of their diseases.

No, not every attending physician is a genius, nor is every race-car driver or concertmaster. But to learn the meaning of the concept, we have to understand the nature of expert performance. One thing we know about the most talented young doctors, drivers and

### ◀ George Washington Carver
**THE PLANT MANAGER**

Has scientific innovation ever appeared under more inhospitable circumstances than attended this man's early years? Born into slavery on a farm in Missouri near the end of the Civil War, Carver was a black man in the Jim Crow South who single-handedly refocused and revitalized the American farm. He pioneered soil analysis, crop management and the control of plant diseases. Carver's research (and his advocacy) provided alternatives—the peanut, the soybean and the pecan—for farmers whose lands lay fallow from the overcultivation of cotton. Though it's not certain that Carver invented peanut butter, he did create more than 300 other products from the humble legume.

### ◀ Leonardo Da Vinci
**THE RENAISSANCE MAN**

At the zenith of the high Renaissance, da Vinci was the embodiment of the aspirations of the age. The small number of his paintings that survive include *The Last Supper* and the *Mona Lisa,* by themselves enough to gain him a place in the pantheon. But in his 67 years, Leonardo was also a sculptor, an architect, an inventor, a botanist, an engineer, a cartographer and much more. His notebooks, written in his distinctive mirror-image handwriting, reveal the workings of a mind whose curiosity knew no bounds and whose breadth is unequaled.

musicians alike is that they rarely materialize like wizards. Someone helps.

That may explain why there aren't as many American geniuses as we'd like. Since well before the administration of George W. Bush began using the impossibly sunny phrase No Child Left Behind, the bureaucrats who write education policy in the U.S. have worried most about kids at the bottom, stragglers of impoverished means or IQs. Surely they are aware, though, that gifted students drop out at the same rate as nongifted kids (about 5%). According to the *Handbook of Gifted Education,* as many as one-fifth of dropouts overall test in the gifted range. In 2007, moreover, Patrick Gonzales of the U.S. Department of Education presented research that showed that the highest-achieving students in six other countries—including Japan, Hungary and Singapore—scored significantly higher in math than their bright U.S. counterparts, who scored about the same as the Estonians—all of which suggests that we are squandering a vital national resource: our best young minds.

American schools spend more than $8 billion a year educating the mentally challenged. Spending on the gifted, meanwhile, isn't even tabulated in some states. By the most generous calculation, we spend no more than $800 million on programs for the gifted. It can't make sense to spend 10 times as much to try to bring low-achieving students to mere proficiency as we do to nurture those with the greatest potential. Whatever the shortcomings of IQ tests, we take for granted that those with scores at least three standard deviations below the mean (that is, 55 or lower) require "special" education. Yet students with IQs

## Aristotle ▶

### THE PHILOSOPHER KING

Of the 200 treatises he wrote, only 31, some of them mere fragments, survive. Yet they show the greatest mind of the classical era, a philosopher scientist whose work, rediscovered in the late Middle Ages, laid the foundations for modern science and still influences how we think about and experience the world. As a naturalist, he was unsurpassed. His *Poetics* was one of the first works of dramatic and literary theory. His ethical pronouncements informed theological discussion in both early Islam and modern Christianity. Okay, so subsequent big thinkers, notably Galileo and Newton, overthrew his view of the universe. Who do you think gave them the intellectual tools for the job?

## ◀ Tim Berners-Lee

### THE WEB MASTER

Berners-Lee is modest about his contribution to the world we live in. "I happened to be in the right place at the right time," he has said. Where he was in 1989 was at CERN, the giant physics laboratory on the Swiss-French border. There, along with his colleagues, he combined the technical building blocks of the World Wide Web: HTML, HTTP (the hypertext transfer protocol) and the www. system for addressing documents. Exactly at 2:56:20 p.m. on Aug. 6, 1991, he posted a message to a newsgroup announcing the WorldWideWeb (WWW) project. One small step for man, one giant step for cat videos (and some other pretty worthwhile stuff too).

that are at least three standard deviations above the mean (145 or higher) often have just as much trouble interacting with average kids. Shouldn't we consider doing something special for them as well? Yes, we are talking about IQs at the extremes: of the 62 million school-age kids in the U.S., only about 62,000 have IQs above 145. (A similar number have IQs below 55.) That's not many, but those included appear in every demographic and in every community. Forget about Binet's subjects; genius doesn't discriminate.

Squandered potential is always tragic, but presumably it is these powerful young minds that, if nourished, could one day cure leukemia or reverse global warming or become the next James Joyce—or at least J.K. Rowling. Unfortunately, in the No Child Left Behind conception of public education—which has been passed on almost effortlessly from Bush to Obama—lifting everyone to a minimum level is more important than allowing students to excel to their potential. It has become more important to identify deficiencies than to cultivate genius. Odd though it seems for a law first enacted during a Republican administration, No Child Left Behind carries a radically egalitarian impulse. In the years since the law was signed in 2002, Illinois has cut more than $16 million from gifted education; Michigan has all but eliminated it save for a token few programs. And federal spending on this line item has declined from $11.3 million in 2002 to $6.7 million in 2013.

STEVE JOBS OFTEN GETS TOSSED ONTO LAYMEN'S lists of geniuses because he helped to create consumer products that seemed unnecessary before their invention but now enjoy constant imitation. (In other

### ◀ Albert Einstein
**THE QUANTUM LEAPER**

Excuse our blatant self-reference, but this does cover things nicely: upon his death in 1955, TIME wrote, "Words could not convey the feelings of a world in which the many unquestioningly accepted Einstein's genius while only the few—and they, of scientific training—adequately understood what he had contributed to knowledge . . . Einstein's only instruments were a pencil and scratch pad; his laboratory was under his cap. Yet he saw farther than a telescope, deeper than a microscope. Einstein traveled in lonely splendor to the crossroads of the visible and the invisible, expressing each in terms of the other." From relativity to the foundations of quantum physics, he was the ultimate thinker of his time, his very surname a synonym for genius.

### ◀ Wolfgang Amadeus Mozart
**THE COMPOSER**

To quote Aaron Copland, Mozart "tapped the source from which all music flows, expressing himself with a spontaneity, refinement and breathtaking rightness that has never since been duplicated." He did it all—more than 600 works, from operas to sonatas to chamber music—in a life that ended far too soon, at 35. Underappreciated while he breathed, he soon cast a giant shadow over his contemporaries and successors; even Beethoven acknowledged the debt. Today, more than 200 years after his death, he remains more popular than ever, acknowledged as maybe the greatest of the classical composers. In Franz Schubert's words, "A world that has produced a Mozart is a world worth saving."

words, his thinking was both original and exemplary.) Now you can use your iPad to Google lists of countless other geniuses—Bach, Tesla, Dante, Goethe, Rembrandt, de Tocqueville, Faulkner, Morrison. Thing is, every one of those lists will reveal cultural and intellectual biases.

Furthermore, until science decides on stricter guidelines for who counts and who doesn't, failures and oddities will continue to dot the landscape of intelligence studies. And will luck and circumstance ever cease being a factor? What might Shakuntala Devi have created if her father hadn't been a circus performer but a Google engineer? In the end, the concept of genius may forever elide that old nature/nurture divide. Scientists now know that genes can be altered during one's lifetime by experiences as routine as long-term cigarette-smoking or overeat-ing; these behaviors can create biological "marks" that help genes to turn on or off. A quick example: you may not be genetically predisposed to lung cancer; instead, if you start smoking when you're 11, it may dial down certain protective genes you'd otherwise carry in abundance, and they won't work as well anymore. In coming years, understanding this "epigenome" will be key to understanding the nature/nurture debate that is already seen as more of a complicated waltz among biology, environmental influence and choice.

From that vantage point, genius ends up looking something like athleticism or sexuality, two other domains in which genes matter but don't rule. Genius requires skill, but it also requires belief. The world's next genius may currently reside in your home, but he or she is not likely to emerge without cultivation.

### ◀ John Coltrane
**THE JAZZ KING**
The saxophone was patented in 1846, in Paris—by, of course, Adolphe Sax. A century later, Coltrane, who grew up in High Point, N.C., took Sax's brassy woodwind in hand and began to produce sounds its inventor had never so much as dreamed of. In music multifaceted and multitonal, 'Trane, who began his career in the twilight days of the Big Band era, discovered and mastered and expanded bebop and hard bop, then lit out for the wild hinterlands of free jazz. Along the way, he composed and recorded some of the most spiritual music ever written—and some of the sexiest.

# MIND OVER MADNESS

BY MAIA SZALAVITZ

*Schizophrenia, bipolar disorder, autism . . .
serious mental illness has the power to both
debilitate and motivate. Behold the tortured genius*

FRETTING ABOUT A COMMUNIST CONSPIRACY LED BY MEN WEARING (OF COURSE) RED TIES OR IMAG-ining that someone is out to poison you seem like anything but the products of a great mind. Yet the first is the delusion of a Nobel laureate, the second the groundless dread of one of the most important artists the world has ever known. The idea of the tortured genius runs deep in Western culture, going back to Aristotle, who wrote that all greatness includes at least a touch of madness. But saying it, even seeing it, is one thing; proving it is quite another. It has been surprisingly difficult for science to show that such a connection, in fact, exists.

For a while now, researchers have noticed some links between the highest ranks of creativity and both bipolar disorder and schizophrenia. A survey of the lives of great musicians, writers and artists, for example, reveals elevated rates of bipolar disorder and sometimes schizophrenia or autistic traits. John Nash was the math whiz who feared those snappily dressed conspirators; his lifelong struggles with paranoid schizophrenia were the subject of the Oscar-winning *A Beautiful Mind*. Pair Vincent van Gogh's fixation about being poisoned with that ear-cutting incident and you have a portrait of a mentally unbalanced painter, perhaps a bipolar one. Sylvia Plath, Virginia Woolf and Ernest Hemingway were all depressives who committed suicide. Georgia O'Keeffe and Abraham Lincoln also wrestled with depression throughout their lives.

Only recently, though, have large studies revealed the same correlation in the population at large. "We validated the idea of a connection between mental illness and creativity," says Simon Kyaga, of Sweden's Karolinska Institute. His team's 40-year study included roughly 1.2 million people—Sweden's extensive medical and professional record-keeping made such far-reaching data-crunching possible—and found that those with bipolar disorder were 8% more likely to have pursued a creative or scientific profession. Conversely, people who had been treated for a variety of other mental conditions, such as depression, ADHD, autism, addictions or schizophrenia, were actually *less* likely to have landed in cre-

**PAINT IT BLACK**
*Vincent van Gogh was
notoriously troubled,
believing men were
out to poison him.*

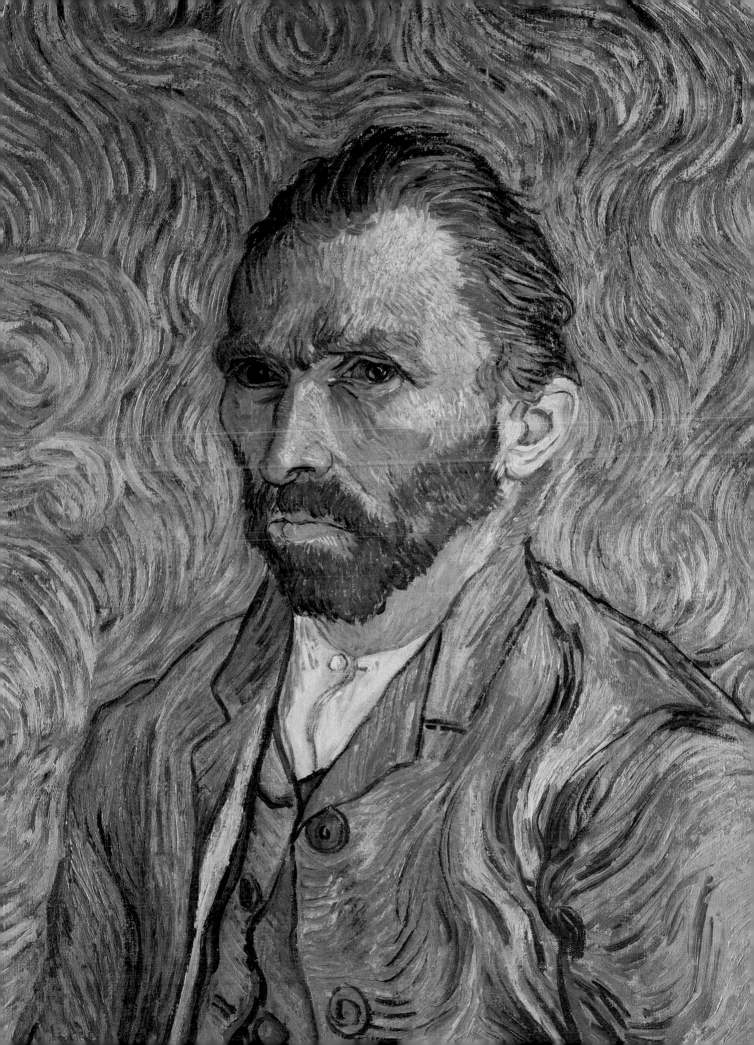

**CALM AND CHAOS** *Nobel Prize winner John Nash solved a classic problem in the field of differential geometry, but he has suffered from paranoid schizophrenia for most of his life.*

ative fields. Authors seemed particularly affected, suffering from both schizophrenia and bipolar disorder at twice the rate of the general population. They had a higher risk of depression, anxiety disorders, addictions and suicide as well.

In fact, Kyaga's was not the first study to find writers to be especially prone to emotional trouble, and although no one has sufficiently explained why this might be so, one theory holds that it is because language itself is intrinsic to some types of insanity. After all, if we can't understand speech, we can't "hear voices." Indeed, one researcher has theorized that schizophrenic genes have withstood the evolutionary test of time despite their obvious downside because they may also be responsible for the human creativity that is the source of language itself.

Aside from writers, however, the connection between mental illness and creativity is actually far stronger in relatives of the afflicted than in the afflicted themselves. Family members of the mentally ill often have some similar tendencies, although typically at levels that don't merit a diagnosis. Those tendencies may be sufficient, though, to ramp up creativity: people whose parents had schizophrenia were 51% more likely to be in a creative profession than those whose parents were unaffected, and those whose parents were bipolar were 33% more likely to be in the arts or sciences. Maybe unusual thoughts and a heightened ability to find links between apparently unrelated ideas, two hallmarks of these brain disorders, provide a fertile ground for imaginative thinking. Maybe people dealing so intimately with these sicknesses develop other outlets for their emotions. In any case, James Joyce and Albert Einstein had children with schizophrenia, and the philosopher and mathematician Bertrand Russell had no fewer than four close relatives with psychotic disorders, including his son.

Kyaga's research uncovered a similar relationship between autism and creativity. Specifically, people who had an autistic sibling were 48% more likely to be scientists and 30% more likely to work in creative fields. Authors once again broke from the pack, twice as likely as others to have had an autistic parent. This developmental disorder has several other strong ties to creativity. First, about 10% of autistic people have "savant skills," that is, exceedingly advanced abilities in calculation, memory, music or art. Think of Raymond Babbitt's card-counting in the film *Rain Man*. Or the real-life feats of autistic author Daniel Tammet, who holds the European record for accurately reciting the most digits of pi: 22,514. It took him five hours and nine minutes.

"The autistic talent is a form of information processing," says Scott Barry Kaufman, an assistant professor of psychology at New York University. "It's an ability for conscious pattern detection and an interest in making sense of complex data, simplifying it to have control over the environment." It follows that the autistic brain is especially conducive to success in math, computer programming, science and music, all disciplines that are built atop complex systems and the patterns within them.

In fact, some experts argue that Einstein and Isaac Newton both had mild forms of the condition. Einstein notoriously didn't talk until he was 4, a delay often seen in autistic people. And those who frequent the world of Internet development and computer programming meet with more than their share of the extreme social awkwardness, repetitive behavior and obsessive focus that characterize autism.

Intensely focused interest and an affinity for repetition, in particular, are symptoms of autistic thought that sync with creativity and heightened achievement. Recent research has found that the factor that most distinguishes ordinariness from great talent is the number of hours of deliberate practice devoted to nurturing that talent, with 10,000 considered the threshold to expert performance. Those with a high tolerance for repetition and an ability to remain on task are obviously far more likely to persist over such an extended period of time.

Indeed, a study found that high creative achievers were twice as likely to make mistakes on a task that required them to shift attention from details to the big picture and vice versa as were those with the lowest level of creative accomplishment. "It's counterintuitive," says the study's lead author, Darya Zabelina, a graduate student, "but people with high creativity perform badly on this test." In similar trials, people with autism or schizophrenia showed equivalent deficits. Chalk up the attention-shifting problems to hyperfocus, which these studies suggest is both a trait of mental disorders and the root of genius-level achievement.

Child prodigies, too, seem to be overrepresented on the autism spectrum. In one study of eight unidentified but well-known prodigies, three qualified for a diagnosis. That's a rate of nearly 40%; autism in the general population hovers at a little over 1%. And all the subjects actually scored higher than people with autism in their level of attention to detail.

It was an impressive group. Among the eight were a child who began speaking at 3 months and was reading by the time he was a year old; two others were reading at 2. One child was programming computers at 3, and one had invented a new discipline of mathematics before reaching puberty. At an age at which most of their peers were finishing preschool, several could reproduce complex pieces of music after hearing them only once, and many had toured internationally or played Carnegie Hall well before they were 10. Yet although most had higher-than-average intelligence, some of their IQs weren't nearly as elevated as their achievements would suggest. One child actually had an IQ of 108, which is only at the high end of normal.

But one thing all the prodigies did have was superior working memory—that is, the ability to actively hold more material in mind at one time. Most of us can easily recall seven digits when we dial the phone, for example. The prodigies could do much better: all were at least in the 99th percentile for working memory. But while excellent working memory may seem like an unqualified gift, research suggests it may also increase the risk for post-traumatic stress disorder. Just as hyperfocus can produce either practiced perfection or useless repetitive behavior, the intense memory that can be a blessing in matters of music or programming can be a curse when it won't let go of the details of, say, a car accident or personal slight.

Of course, suffering isn't always a side effect of genius; many highly gifted people are no more likely to have issues than anyone else. In fact, as the author of the prodigy study, Joanne Ruthsatz of Ohio State University, points out, other research has shown that people with high IQs are generally less prone to mental illness. "People like to look for flaws," she says. "They talk about prodigies like they must be weird. But they're actually wonderful, warm and altruistic."

Extreme gifts, though, are often enough double-edged swords: prolonged focus can get you to Carnegie Hall if it's applied at the keyboard, but it can leave you unskilled if it has you staring at a spinning wheel. A brilliant working memory may help to devise elegant algorithms, but it can also debilitate by turning unpleasant experiences into traumatic ones. And the fevered peaks of mania can birth original insights and otherworldly art, but they can also have you believing you're the planet's savior. Genius arises only if the wild sparks of creativity don't incinerate their vessel first.

**FIGURES HEAD** *Autistic author Daniel Tammet holds the European record for accurately reciting the most digits of pi: 22,514. In 2004, the feat took five hours and nine minutes.*

# SPEAK OF THE DEVIL

**BY JEFFREY KLUGER**

*They overpopulate our fiction, but in real life, evil geniuses are, thankfully, a very rare breed*

**COLD STARE** *Nazi minister of propaganda Joseph Goebbels glared up at the camera—and more specifically, at the photographer who wielded it in 1933.*

THERE WAS A TIME WHEN JOSEPH GOEBBELS might have passed as normal—before his bilious ideas began to spew forth, before his work as Adolf Hitler's propaganda minister put the power of language behind the poison of Nazism, before his face became synonymous with history's most hateful regime. That time was also before most people got a good look at him. And then, in 1933, they did—thanks to a very particular photograph taken by a very particular photographer.

In September of that year the world was still at relative peace, and Goebbels, along with a delegation from the new Nazi government of Germany, traveled to Geneva, Switzerland, to attend a meeting of the League of Nations. Dark-suited dignitaries gathered in the garden of the Carlton Hotel, and photographers from global news organizations moved freely among them. One of the cameramen in attendance was the not-yet-legendary Alfred Eisenstaedt, then just 34, who was born in Prussia, moved to Berlin and had already established himself as a photographer with an artist's eye. He was also a Jew. Somewhere in the sunny garden, Eisenstaedt spotted Goebbels sitting in a chair, attended by his private secretary and an interpreter, as he prepared for a radio address he was about to deliver. More to the point, Goebbels spotted Eisenstaedt in return.

Goebbels had been smiling at someone, but when his eyes shifted to Eisenstaedt, any trace of sociability fell away. Perhaps Goebbels knew who—and what—Eisenstaedt was. Perhaps he guessed; perhaps Eisenstaedt himself projected something—fear, distaste, alarm. Whatever the case, Goebbels was suddenly transformed, and in that instant, Eisenstaedt's shutter snapped.

What the photographer captured was the image of a small and skeletal man—"a seething homunculus," as Life.com editor Ben Cosgrove would memorably put it 80 years later—sitting rigidly, head inclined slightly toward the camera, eyes looking icily into it. A crease runs down Goebbels's left cheek like a cutlass scar, and his hands, talonlike, grip the arms of his chair, a folded piece of paper clasped in the left. Here was the look of a deeply evil man, a man whose fast-clicking brain and seductive command of language also made him a very intelligent one. The combination would soon cost the world dearly.

The mind ought to rebel at the idea of the evil genius. The very nature of genius, after all, should be rare and wonderful. But evil genius does exist—even if not always in the form we conjure. In popular iconography, it is the mad scientist or criminal mastermind who most commonly personifies the idea, but in truth, those characters are extremely unusual. Science requires a surpassing patience and maturity of thought that are simply not consistent with the bloody appetites of the truly evil. And criminal masterminds? Name one. John Gotti? Al Capone? The fictitious Tony Soprano? Mere bullies. They may share a kind of nefarious creativity, but in the end they are defined by little more than their ability to inspire fear.

Even Osama bin Laden fails the evil-genius test. At best, he was a well-organized nihilist. In the terrible wake of Sept. 11, we tried to make the late al Qaeda leader out to be more than he was. "See how he got our attention with the first plane, then sent the second one into the other tower when he knew we'd all be watching?" the media asked in awe—as if the amateur pilots at the sticks of the hijacked aircraft, after seizing control of two different planes at two different times, could have somehow gotten them to converge at a particular moment even if they'd wanted to. Bin Laden may have been the author of the tragedy, but any damn fool can knock down a skyscraper. You want to show a little genius? Try building one.

Real evil genius needs to have a certain sweep and scale. And it must move people to do what they might not otherwise have done. Bin Laden's murderous masterpiece may have boosted al Qaeda recruitment a bit, but the only true army he motivated was the global coalition that drove him into hiding. Until history proves otherwise, then, the only legitimate candidates for evil genius are political figures who have what amounts to a nation under their control.

Most of the world's great bloodbaths have been the result of a leader understanding—and ingeniously exploiting—the line human beings draw between insiders and outsiders, between the familiar tribe and the alien other. Volumes have been written about what goes on in the collective mind of places like Nazi Germany or the collapsing Yugoslavia, where genocide was national policy. While killers like Hitler or Slobodan Milosevic can never be put on the couch, we can understand the xenophobic strings they played in their people. "Yugoslavia is the great modern example of manipulating tribal sentiments to create mass murder," says Jonathan Haidt, a social psychologist at New York University. "You saw it in Rwanda, too. In most cases of genocide, you have a moral entrepreneur who exploits tribalism for evil purposes."

Those exceedingly bad men are well known: Pol Pot, who set Cambodia's ostensibly pure-minded rural citizens against the educated urbanites and used that manufactured divide to slaughter 1.7 million innocents during the reign of the Khmer Rouge in the 1970s; Mao Zedong, who exploited the same kind of "class struggle" schism to stoke and justify China's Cultural Revolution in the 1960s, which saw 1.5 million deaths; Ismael Enver, one of the leaders of Ottoman Turkey, who was responsible for the murder of 1.5 million Armenians in 1915.

But it is by no means just body count that's the measure of evil genius. Up to 1.2 million soldiers and hundreds of thousands of civilians died in the eight-year Iran-Iraq war, but although Saddam Hussein was evil, he was no one's idea of a genius—more vulgar thug than anything else. Iran's Ayatollah Khomeini, with the despot's bloodlust cloaked in the pious guise of the cleric, was much closer to the real deal.

No, the true measure of evil genius is not the ability to motivate large numbers merely to kill but to motivate them to savor doing it. That goes beyond inspiring what psychologist Robert Sternberg, president of the University of Wyoming, calls "hot hate," a deep and visceral loathing of the outsider. Instead, evil genius traffics in "cold hate," a more deliberate state of mind that leads to a cognitive, intellectualized decision to act—to build the concentration camps, buy the gas, run the rail lines, burn the bodies... and to do it all while remaining convinced that your actions are not only historically justifiable but socially virtuous.

The worst currents of history have always produced leaders who are able to persuade otherwise humane people to do deeply inhumane things. It is left to the rest of us to remain aware of that danger. "We are responsible for our incredulity," wrote Samantha Power, President Obama's pick for U.N. ambassador, in *A Problem from Hell,* her book about genocide. By believing our eyes when we see horror happening, we can stop the bloodshed before it begins.

# GENIUS AT WORK

# THEY CAN DO THE MATH

BY MICHAEL LEMONICK

*In the end, the mind of a scientific genius may be unknowable. But at least we can check their work*

ONGTIME RESIDENTS OF PRINCETON, N.J., STILL LOVE TO TELL STORIES ABOUT ALBERT EINSTEIN, who lived in the town for the last few decades of his life. One concerns the time the great physicist discovered that the light switch in his living room had stopped working. He called a local electrician, who came over, fiddled with the wires for a few minutes, then proclaimed the job finished. "You," declared Einstein, flipping the switch on and off with delight, "are a genius!"

Which goes to show that "genius" is a word thrown around quite loosely—even by those who should know one. To be fair, experts who study the phenomenon can't really nail down "genius" either. And that's true even in fields like science and math, the measurable achievements of which you'd think would make the concept easier to define. Howard Gardner, the Harvard psychologist who has championed the idea that intelligence comes in different flavors and thus isn't always quantifiable by an IQ test, acknowledges this apparent mushiness. In his book *Extraordinary Minds,* Gardner writes, "It is conceivable that extraordinary individuals lead lives that are so distinctive that no generalizations can emerge from intensive studies of their particular wrinkles."

That hasn't stopped students of scientific genius from trying to make those generalizations. The late British psychologist Raymond Cattell, for example, determined that famous scientists tend to be withdrawn. He cited among others the physicist Henry Cavendish, who figured out how to calculate the weight of the Earth in 1798

$$uation:$$
$$z^n$$
$$n \ has \ no$$
$$integers$$

but was evidently so fearful of social interaction that upon being asked to meet a guest at a state function to which he'd been dragged, he ran down the corridor, "squeaking like a bat."

Here are some other peculiarities that researchers have isolated in their attempts to figure out what makes scientific savants tick: columbiphilia (love of pigeons), kakiphobia (fear of dirt), scotophilia (love of the dark), pathophobia (fear of germs), spereophobia (fear of round objects), triphilia (obsession with the number three), dipteraphobia (fear of flies), claustrophilia (love of confined spaces), thermophilia (love of hot spots) and visual and auditory hallucinations. That just about settles things, doesn't it?

More helpfully, high achievers in science, like those in other walks of life, are more likely than average Joes and Janes to have lost a parent, and some researchers believe that birth order can affect one's chances of being a genius (firstborns have a leg up). Similarly, being uprooted from one's traditional culture might also raise the odds.

There is, though, one obvious flaw in each of these lines of reasoning. "There exist hundreds, maybe even thousands, of dimensions in which people may vary," says Dean Keith Simonton, a psychologist and genius expert at the University of California, Davis. Purely by chance, some of those dimensions will be more genius-friendly, others pretty much irrelevant.

**SOMETHING TO PROVE**
*Andrew Wiles cracked Fermat's Last Theorem in 1995. The problem, which he first pondered as a boy, had stumped others for 350 years.*

It's not even clear what the benchmarks are for geniuses. Do they have to come up with an idea that changes the world? Is one such idea enough? If not, how many are needed exactly? Was Edison a genius because he invented such an astonishing range of world-changing technologies (including, by the way, talking dolls)? Or does he lose points because the ideas and their execution frequently came from those working for him?

Scan the list of Nobel Prize winners in scientific disciplines, and you see that some were lauded for dazzling insights and others for doing clever but not especially brilliant experiments. Still others stumbled on their game-changing discoveries purely by accident, as Alexander Fleming did with penicillin and Robert Wilson and Arno Penzias did when they found remnant light from the Big Bang.

Given all the various measures of genius, the saf-

**TOP DRAWER** *With a few strikingly clear diagrams, physicist Richard Feynman described subatomic particle interactions.*

est bet might be the two-part definition concocted by the late Mark Kac, a brilliant Polish-American mathematician, when he tried to explain the gifts of the physicist Richard Feynman, who died in 1988. "There are two kinds of geniuses," wrote Kac, "the 'ordinary' and the 'magicians.' An ordinary genius is a fellow whom you and I would be just as good as, if we were only many times better. There is no mystery as to how his mind works. . . . It is different with the magicians. Even after we understand what they have done, it is completely dark. Richard Feynman is a magician of the highest caliber."

One thing that distinguished Feynman was the way he came at problems from an unexpected direction, guided more by personal intuition than anything else. His scheme of simple diagrams to represent subatomic particle interactions, for example, made thorny problems in the esoteric world of quantum physics far easier and more intuitive to understand. It helped that Feynman's mind was more restless than most; he speculated about all manner of things—including nanotechnology, parallel computing and quantum computing—decades before they became hot areas of research in science and technology.

Intuition, though, rarely leads anywhere if it isn't partnered with an obsessive need to follow it relentlessly—and that's one characteristic that true geniuses inevitably possess. "They are distinguished," writes Simonton, "by their intense devotion to their work. In fact, their careers assume the quality of creative crusades."

Einstein began his journey to the Special Theory of Relativity by wondering what it would be like to take a ride on a beam of light. If he'd simply concluded that, wow, it would be really awesome, rather than laboring tirelessly over his computations for years, he would never have gotten to E=mc². Geniuses, writes Simonton, are no better than the rest of us at avoiding false starts and missteps; it's their perseverance that differentiates them: "Scientific geniuses are right so often only because they are willing to make numerous mistakes, which, fortunately for their reputations, posterity is inclined to forget."

Back to Einstein. He spent the last decade or two of his life laboring to produce a "unified field theory" that would tie the forces of electromagnetism and gravity into a single set of equations. He never accomplished that, but in a strange double twist, what he declared to be his greatest blunder—a prediction of an antigravity force in those original equations of relativity—may exist after all as what is now called "dark

**IDEA MACHINE** *How big was Thomas Edison's brain? The Wizard of Menlo Park was the holder of more than 1,000 patents, including those for the phonograph, the motion picture camera and, of course, the incandescent lamp.*

energy." The only thing Einstein was wrong about was being wrong.

A more recent instance of brilliance coupling with obsession is Oxford professor Andrew Wiles's proof of Fermat's Last Theorem, a problem that had remained unsolved for more than 300 years. Undaunted by the generations of mathematicians who had failed, Wiles reportedly first decided to tackle it when he was just 10 years old. After he began to attack it in earnest, at 33, it took another seven years of secret labor in an attic room. (Knowing how quixotic the task was, Wiles told no one but his wife what he was up

to.) He finally cracked it in 1993. When a crucial step in his reasoning turned out to be incorrect, he went back for another year to fix it, confirming Simonton's theory: *Scientific geniuses are right so often only because they are willing to make numerous mistakes, which, fortunately for their reputations, posterity is inclined to forget.*

In many cases, including those of Wiles and Feynman, dazzlingly insightful solutions come from outside the box; sometimes—see Einstein—they come from a patent clerk without any distinguished track record in physics. You might expect, therefore, that

**KERNELS OF TRUTH** *With a few ears of corn, Barbara McClintock convinced the many skeptics in the world of genetics that genes can not only be switched on and off, they can also jump from one chromosome to another.*

the keepers of a realm as hypercritical as science would take a good long while to accept them. Yet the work of these three men was accepted at once, or at least taken quite seriously, because each could demonstrate it mathematically. Equations don't lie—either they add up or they don't.

World-changing insights aren't always so obvious, though, as the case of geneticist Barbara McClintock makes clear. In the 1940s, McClintock became convinced by a series of corn-breeding experiments that genes alone couldn't explain the wide variation within species or from one species to another. The genome, she argued, had to include some sort of molecular switches that turned genes on in certain situations and off in others. Moreover, she reasoned, genes could not be fixed in place; rather, they could "jump" from one chromosome to another, which would lead to an even wider range of genetic variation.

Her colleagues, she once told TIME, thought she was "crazy, absolutely mad." Eventually she stopped

# HISTORY'S SCIENTIFIC GENIUSES WEREN'T JUST BRILLIANT; THEY WERE AHEAD OF THEIR TIME.

publishing her research because nobody was willing to pay it any mind. Then, years later, genetics finally caught up with her. In 1983, McClintock won the Nobel Prize in Physiology or Medicine, the first woman to win that award solo.

McClintock, unlike Feynman and Einstein, was what Kac would call an "ordinary genius." Sure, she was off-the-charts smart, but her discoveries, at least in theory, could have been made by someone else.

Of course, they weren't—and that's another aspect of genius that experts are quick to note. When Einstein came up with Special and General Relativity Theory, the latter proved especially difficult for even eminent physicists of his day to understand. Today, tens of thousands of college students master it (more or less) every year. Einstein and Newton and Galileo and history's other scientific geniuses weren't just brilliant; they were also ahead of their time.

Sometimes, though, not by much. In many cases, a leap in thought—what the philosopher of science Thomas Kuhn labeled a "paradigm shift" and Harvard's Gardner says "gives the rest of us a new way of understanding the world and building upon that understanding"—blooms from a field already in ferment.

Galileo and Newton made enormous leaps in explaining the laws of the universe, for example, at a time when the age-old idea that the sun revolves around the Earth was becoming untenable. Einstein came up with Special Relativity because the physicists who preceded him had begun to uncover the electromagnetic nature of light. Evolution by natural selection arose as the answer to why Earth came to have such an abundance of species, a question very much in the air in Darwin's time. If any of those paradigm shifters had lived in a different time or had a different sort of education, maybe they still would have made great breakthroughs. Or maybe they wouldn't.

One notable exception to this right-place-right-time model is the great Indian mathematician Srinivasa Ramanujan. In the early years of the 20th century, with almost no formal training, the young

Ramanujan worked in near-isolation, filling notebook after notebook with mathematical notions. Wholly ignorant of what was and wasn't known at the time, Ramanujan re-proved theorems that other mathematicians had already figured out, but he also came up with hundreds of new results that are still being analyzed today. Ramanujan, who died at 32 in 1920, would have been recognized as a genius pretty much wherever or whenever he lived.

Ramanujan's field of pure mathematics, though, is one of the few in which a single person can still make fundamental discoveries. Much of science and technology has become a group endeavor. "Remember when the Higgs Boson was verified?" says Gard-

**SELF-TAUGHT** *Despite little formal education, Srinivasa Ramanujan solved a number of complex theorems on his own.*

ner. That was done, he points out, by two research groups, each comprising dozens upon dozens of individuals. James Watson and Francis Crick discovered the structure of DNA more or less by themselves, although they got key clues from the work of others. But the Human Genome Project, which sequenced our DNA, involved hundreds of researchers all over the world.

We will never run out of scientific geniuses; whatever mix of intelligence, drive and imagination is responsible for that extraordinary class of thinker is deeply embedded in our genes. But we might find it increasingly hard to single out the stars from the rest of the team.— WITH REPORTING BY DAVID BJERKLIE

# RANKING THE TECH TITANS

BY HARRY McCRACKEN

*Which ones made the real breakthroughs—and who merely stood on the shoulders of others?*

Summoning the names of the icons of past technological revolutions is easy: Edison, Bell, Tesla, Wright, Kodak's George Eastman, Polaroid's Edwin Land. But the closer the roll call gets to the present, the tougher it is to identify figures in the technology sector who can join the roster of geniuses without stirring up debate.

The late Steve Jobs may be the nearest example of an unassailable modern-day, household-name genius, bolstered by his portfolio of more than 30 years of industry-redefining products from the Apple II to the iPod to the iPad. Surely if he'd never been born, these landmark innovations wouldn't exist, at least not in exactly the form we know them. Yet some critics grumble that those successes were nothing more than highly polished takes on already-dreamed-up concepts rather than original, from-the-ground-up inventions.

Wherever you fall on Jobs, once you look past him, there does seem to be an alarming scarcity of current candidates for technological genius status. But let's pause a moment before concluding that's a doomsday sign that we humans are getting stupider and less creative. For starters, there are in fact plenty of bonafide genius-caliber inventors of the traditional sort alive and tinkering today. They just need to spring for some better representation. It's no surprise, for example, if the names Martin Cooper and Steven Sasson don't ring any bells. But it is a shame. In the 1970s, Cooper invented the cell phone and Sasson devised the first digital camera. These guys should have elementary schools named after them and statues erected in public squares.

If the 84-year-old Cooper and 63-year-old Sasson are the elder statesmen of

**BIG SHOTS**
*The digital age propelled innovators like (from top) Apple's Steve Jobs and Facebook's Mark Zuckerberg into stardom, making them household names.*

epoch-shifting innovation, then Ren Ng, at 33, is the new kid. In 2006, Ng wrote his Stanford dissertation on light-field technology, an arcane science that captures light waves in three dimensions, thus allowing for nifty tricks such as refocusing a photo after it has been taken. He turned his research into a start-up, Lytro, that released a $399 camera based on his technology in 2012. Consumer light-field photography is just getting started, but it wouldn't be anything at all if Ng hadn't tackled the challenge. His inventiveness is very much in the classic mold of the great technologists of the past.

Sasson, Cooper and Ng have something particular in common: they created physical stuff. That kind of development was once the norm, most major breakthroughs resulting in something tangible. Thomas Edison figured out a way to keep a carbon filament illuminated, and we got the lightbulb. Alexander Bell found a new way to summon Mr. Watson, and we got the telephone. Orville Wright kept a flying machine aloft for 120 feet, and we got interminable airport security lines. Their creations are there for all to see.

In the digital age, though, innovation is frequently ethereal and therefore less evocative. In late 1992 and early 1993, Marc Andreessen and Eric Bina of the University of Illinois Urbana-Champaign's National Center for Supercomputer Applications invented Mosaic, the first fully graphical web browser. It's as influential a piece of consumer technology as any developed in the past half-century. But devising a program that displays bitmapped images alongside HTML-formatted text isn't the sort of accomplishment that makes for iconic photo ops and memorable anecdotes.

Further, like Jobs and most of today's top-tier technologists, Andreessen and Bina didn't start with a blank slate. Mosaic was an improved version of a browser that Tim Berners-Lee, who invented the World Wide Web at the CERN research lab in Geneva, Switzerland, had created not long before. Berners-Lee's brainchild was itself built atop a couple of decades' worth of predecessor Internet technologies. (It also happened to run initially on a computer made by NeXT, the company founded by Jobs after he was thrown out of Apple in 1985.)

Today, nearly every technical breakthrough will one day be a building block for future breakthroughs, and they in turn will be building blocks themselves. The bigger the construction set gets, the easier it is to do and make amazing things. That's great for inventive types and for the public. But it does decrease the chances of a brainiac's inspiration springing out of nowhere to dazzle the planet.

Anyway, as Edison could attest, if wizards want to dazzle, they need a strong entrepreneurial streak. Growing up, Mark Zuckerberg was by all accounts a programming prodigy, and that definitely helped him hack out the first version of what he called "The Facebook" in his Harvard dorm in 2004. But if Zuck is fodder for this discussion, it's because he founded and runs a company that now reaches more than a billion people a month. That feat has relatively little to do with his technical chops and everything to do with his vision, determination and agility as a corporate leader.

Does that argue against Zuckerberg being an exceptional thinker? Of course not, especially when

**COMPUTER WHIZ** *Marc Andreessen cofounded the first widely used web browser, Mosaic, as well as the more commonly known Netscape.*

you consider that Friendster, MySpace and their now irrelevant cousins had a head start on the basic Facebook premise, and none of them changed the world.

In fact, although it seems contradictory, maybe today's dizzying pace of innovation has actually stunted any potential bumper crop in geniuses. An awful lot of interesting creations have had finite shelf lives, and their creators, whose intellects seemed superhuman when their products debuted, have also been remaindered.

Here are some bright minds heading major technology companies today: Zuckerberg; Larry Page and Sergey Brin (Google); Jeff Bezos (Amazon); Jack Dorsey (Square); Marissa Mayer (Yahoo!). Does a genius walk among them? It's not for us to say. We may know who the geniuses of past generations were, but we must leave it to future generations to identify our own.

# THE PICTURE
# OF LEADERSHIP

BY JEFFREY KLUGER

*Winning votes and governing nations are quite different skills. Through the years, political genius has helped the best leaders do both*

THE MOST EXTRAORDINARY PICTURES YOU'VE EVER SEEN OF FRANKLIN ROOSEVELT HAVE NOTHING to do with the equally extraordinary things he did in his official capacity as president. Yes, there are press photos of him signing Social Security into law, resolutely addressing Congress the day after the shock of the Pearl Harbor attacks, negotiating with the Allied leaders as the world descended into war—and they are important moments all. But the truly, if subtly, remarkable shots are the ones that show him doing nothing more than standing up.

Roosevelt, who was elected president at 50 and served until his death at 63, never stood unassisted after the summer of 1921 when, at 39, he contracted what was in his case the incongruously named infantile paralysis, or polio. Suddenly, the rising star of the Democratic Party—its vice presidential nominee in 1920—was being dispatched to the political wilderness, a tragic figure confined to a wheelchair, who would spend the rest of his life quietly tending his family's fortune at his Hudson River estate. It's a matter of historical record that that's not quite how things turned out: FDR came back to win two terms as governor of New York and a stunning four as president of the United States, becoming one of the most consequential people ever to hold the office. He owed that resurrection, in part, to his ability to create illusion.

When Roosevelt stood to deliver a speech, his legs were locked rigid by braces concealed by his trousers as his hands grabbed hold of the lectern. To the unsuspecting, he looked the picture of a strong and upright leader. When he waved from a balcony or ship's deck, one hand would grip the rail or, discreetly, the arm of a military aide. He rose to throw out first pitches on opening days of the baseball season the same way. When the cameras finished snapping and the moment was past, his entourage closed around him to help him down. It was all deft image-making of a sort that, in the modern era, would surely not be necessary. His wasn't the modern era, however, but one in which a man who presumed to lead had best be able-bodied. So Roosevelt, who was not above a bit of legerdemain, hap-

**RISING ABOVE** *Even with his handicap, FDR projected a convincing strength that won over American voters again and again.*

**GREAT COMMUNICATOR** *President Ronald Reagan (center right, with Mikhail Gorbachev in 1988) was as skilled at selling his policies as he was at implementing them.*

ponents, was in some ways Roosevelt's equal.

It's the single-talented theorists, though the ones who dream up big ideas, write them down in private and then release them to the world—who give all the other political geniuses something to work with in the first place. Aristotle, who lived in the fourth century B.C., provided an armature for all political systems to follow. He articulated most clearly the idea of the city and the citizen, and the value—even the moral imperative—of civic participation. It was he who first (or at least best) argued for the vibrancy of democracies and the advantages of a system that does not confer power on only an elite class. "Any member of the assembly, taken separately, is certainly inferior to the wise man," Aristotle wrote in *Politics.* "But the state is made up of many individuals. And as a feast to which all the guests contribute is better than a banquet furnished by a single man, so a multitude is a better judge of many things than any individual."

Sometimes it takes a while for claims of genius to be either validated or revealed as a sham. What Karl Marx had to say once sounded awfully good to a lot of people, and when czarist Russia and then nationalist China tumbled for him, it seemed as if the seminal Communist knew what he was talking about. A few more decades, though, exposed the holes in his thinking, leaving little in the modern Marxist trophy case beyond the twin disasters of Cuba and North Korea.

Edmund Burke, on the other hand, has survived into the 21st century with his portfolio of ideas, though periodically battered, more or less intact. Burke is the

pily assumed an able-bodied pose. Was it dishonest? Sure. But it was also ingenious.

Political genius takes many forms. There is the genius of the theorist and that of the image-maker; the genius of the strategist and the dealmaker and the speech-giver. Sometimes threads converge. FDR, with his sweeping vision for a remade nation and an uncanny ability to get much of it implemented while winning serial landslides, had multiple talents at his disposal. More recently, Ronald Reagan, with his clear-eyed worldview, phenomenal popular appeal and a similar ability to strike bargains with op-

18th-century British politician with a resistance to all but gradual societal change and a deep belief in the primacy of property and the naturally hierarchical nature of society, who is seen as the father of modern conservatism. There is a certain pitilessness to Burke's ideas, which in some ways makes them better suited to the period in which he first set them out. But the high times conservatism enjoyed in both the U.S. and the U.K. during the 1980s and 1990s reintroduced Burke as a powerfully relevant figure. The uncertain time conservatives are having in both countries now is just a reminder of the shortcomings of his thinking. "On the one hand," Winston Churchill once wrote, Burke "is revealed as a foremost apostle of liberty, on the other the redoubtable champion of authority." Squaring that circle was never going to be easy.

Churchill himself makes nearly everybody's short list of political geniuses. First elected to public office as a member of Parliament from the constituency of Oldham in 1900, he wasn't finally pried out of politics until 55 years later, after completing a second term as prime minister and making stops as Chancellor of the Exchequer, First Lord of the Admiralty, Home Secretary, Secretary of State for Air, Secretary of State for War and more. It wasn't just that Churchill was tireless (though he was) or a brilliant tactician (though he was that, too). It was that he seemed to be present at and intimately involved in all of the U.K.'s pivot points in the late-19th and early- to mid-20th centuries: modernizing the British armed forces, arguing the Conservative economic cause while battling its stubborn protectionism, helping to rebuild the country after World War I, winning World War II, rebuilding again and leading his people in the early, volatile years of the Cold War. Churchill's gift was his adaptability—his talent for fathoming the needs and exigencies of so many different eras and finding

**PROBLEM SOLVER**
*Winston Churchill ably guided Great Britain through dark times.*

solutions to problems that were unique to their times.

What Churchill was to the waning British empire, Deng Xiaoping was to the rising power of China. If there is any true genius in the long, convoluted history of postrevolutionary China, it is Deng, who joined the Communist Party in 1924, participated in the celebrated Long March in 1934 and rose to power as part of Mao Zedong's inner circle. But like so many others, he was denounced during the Cultural Revolution that began in 1966, and three years later he was sent to the countryside to labor in a tractor factory. Deng, however, could read the shifting winds. By the early 1970s, Mao was a spent force, the Cultural Revolution had been exposed as the murderous mess it was, and Deng, who was never one of its supporters, felt free to repudiate it openly. This won him popular favor, especially after the political purge of the Gang of Four (led by Mao's wife Jiang Qing), who were behind many of the excesses of the 1960s.

Deng maneuvered his way back into power, and in 1975, just six years after he had been assigned to building farm equipment, he was the dignitary welcoming visiting American president Gerald Ford. By 1982, he was the supreme leader of the country and in that capacity initiated the opening of the Chinese economy that, just three decades later, has made the world's most populous nation also one of its richest and most powerful.

American presidents rarely travel such a tortuous route to power—though Richard Nixon's 1968 redemption following defeats in the 1960 presidential election and the 1962 California gubernatorial race does have a certain whipsaw quality to it. Alas, Nixon was no political genius, as his sorry end proved. Bill Clinton, however, arguably is.

Clinton was not a transformational president—partly because the peaceful and prosperous years in which he governed called for no grand transformation, and partly because his constant tacking to please the polls made him too cautious by half. But he was and remains the most natural, innate politician of the modern American era—and maybe of any American era. It is a truth endlessly repeated that to chat even briefly with Clinton in a crowded room was to come away convinced that he found you

the most interesting and consequential person he'd met all day. The ubiquity of the observation does not diminish its truth. That intoxicating charm—played out both at the retail level and before national TV audiences—is part of what has allowed him to survive serial scandals, any one of which would have sunk a lesser politician.

Abraham Lincoln was an entirely different species of leader. He is America's most lionized president, but the hagiography that surrounds him makes it impossible to assess him accurately. Still, his extraordinary ability to herd the wild cats that surrounded him—his fractious Cabinet, a feral Congress, a nation that had torn itself apart—knows no presidential parallel. That, combined with high principle that was more goodness than brilliance, easily earns him his historic acclaim. Was Lincoln a genius? Sure—but it was just part of a larger suite of gifts.

Thomas Jefferson's restless wizardry was of the polymath variety: architect, inventor, agronomist,

**REDEMPTION SONG** *Deng Xiaoping maneuvered his way back into power, then put the People's Republic of China on the path to prosperity.*

**PEOPLE'S CHAMP** *President Clinton's genius didn't lie in his ability to pass transformational legislation, but rather in his affable demeanor and natural political acumen. His charm cast a spell, both face-to-face and before TV audiences.*

astronomer, political theorist. For him, too, the presidency may have been but a component of the whole. Dwight Eisenhower was manifestly a military mastermind—the mammoth undertaking that was D-Day alone is more than enough to earn him that honorific. But he was an uninspiring, anodyne politician—though, as was the case with Clinton, the times needed him only to be good, not great. Reagan *was* great. Even people who disagreed with his policies marveled at his ability to sell them and strike deals to implement them. John Kennedy? A tragic incomplete.

And what of Barack Obama? The jury, surely, is still out on the current president, as history and simple fairness dictate it must be, until his time in office is over and his works can be considered with some distance. The first African American president in a nation that can still be riven by race was always going to have to be an exceptional person, and had Obama not come along when he did, there's no telling when that historical milestone would have been crossed.

Some physicists argue that, while the Theory of General Relativity and the other great insights of Albert Einstein would eventually have been arrived at even if the great man himself had not done so, he hastened that progress by a good 50 years. It's probably an exaggeration to say that without Obama, an African American would not have occupied the Oval Office until 2058, but his particular blend of raw intelligence, preternatural calm and brilliant oratory surely helped speed the march of history. Clearly he was helped by his team of strategists, who dramatically elevated the art of getting out the vote, microtargeting precisely defined electoral blocs and using social media for fundraising, messaging and more. Their genius papers have been stamped; their boss's remain in the pending pile.

That makes sense, because history serves up politicians a lot more often than it serves up political geniuses. Every country needs a leader, and all governmental systems have their philosophers and thinkers. The ones who soar—who transform their nations or move the whole world—emerge unpredictably, and yet often just when we need them. Whether it's good fortune that produces them or circumstances that nudge them into the breach is impossible to say. However they arrive in our midst, we are better for their work—and should be grateful for the time we have them.

# WHAT'S SO FUNNY?

BY JAMES PONIEWOZIK

*Truth in art? Stephen Colbert finds truth in 'truthiness.' If that isn't exactly Picasso-esque, it does make him a creative genius for our time*

THERE ARE AS MANY KINDS OF ARTISTIC BRILLIANCE AS THERE ARE KINDS OF ART. THERE IS THE kind that stares at a slab of stone and sees what parts need to fall away to reveal the muscular contours of a human figure, and the kind that can evoke in the thrumming of a guitar the sound of train wheels as they roll by a lonesome convict in Folsom Prison.

But there's also the kind that realizes that the world and the way we see it have changed so drastically that we need a new means to capture it. Think of the Renaissance artists who introduced linear perspective in their paintings; think James Joyce and Virginia Woolf, who pioneered stream-of-consciousness fiction; think Bob Dylan going electric. And think Stephen Colbert, a satirist whose subject—the media and political culture—had seemingly moved beyond the reach of satire.

Before the 2005 debut of *The Colbert Report*, on which the star nightly plays a blow-dried blowhard of a cable opinionator, there were plenty of TV news send-ups, from *Network* to *Saturday Night Live* to *The Simpsons*'s oily anchorman Kent Brockman. But those were all spoofs for an earlier time, when the tag team of network anchors and local newsreaders ruled. In the cable era, news has become something more massive and unwieldy: a nonstop, ratings-amped mediasphere of pontification and provocation in which personality trumps competence and passion trumps fact.

It was during the second term of George W. Bush that a presidential adviser speaking anonymously to reporter Ron Suskind pooh-poohed "the reality-based community . . . who believe that solutions emerge from your judicious study of discernible reality." Instead, the aide continued, "we're an empire now, and when we act, we create our own reality." Meanwhile, the most popular cable news hosts were Bill O'Reilly and Keith Olbermann, warehouses of argument who loaded up their fans' ideological shopping carts with talking points.

Such an already extreme situation could never be adequately spoofed by a two-hour

**LISTEN UP**
*Over the past decade, Colbert has tirelessly parlayed his late-night blowhard news persona into a full-fledged movement, becoming one of America's most important voices along the way.*

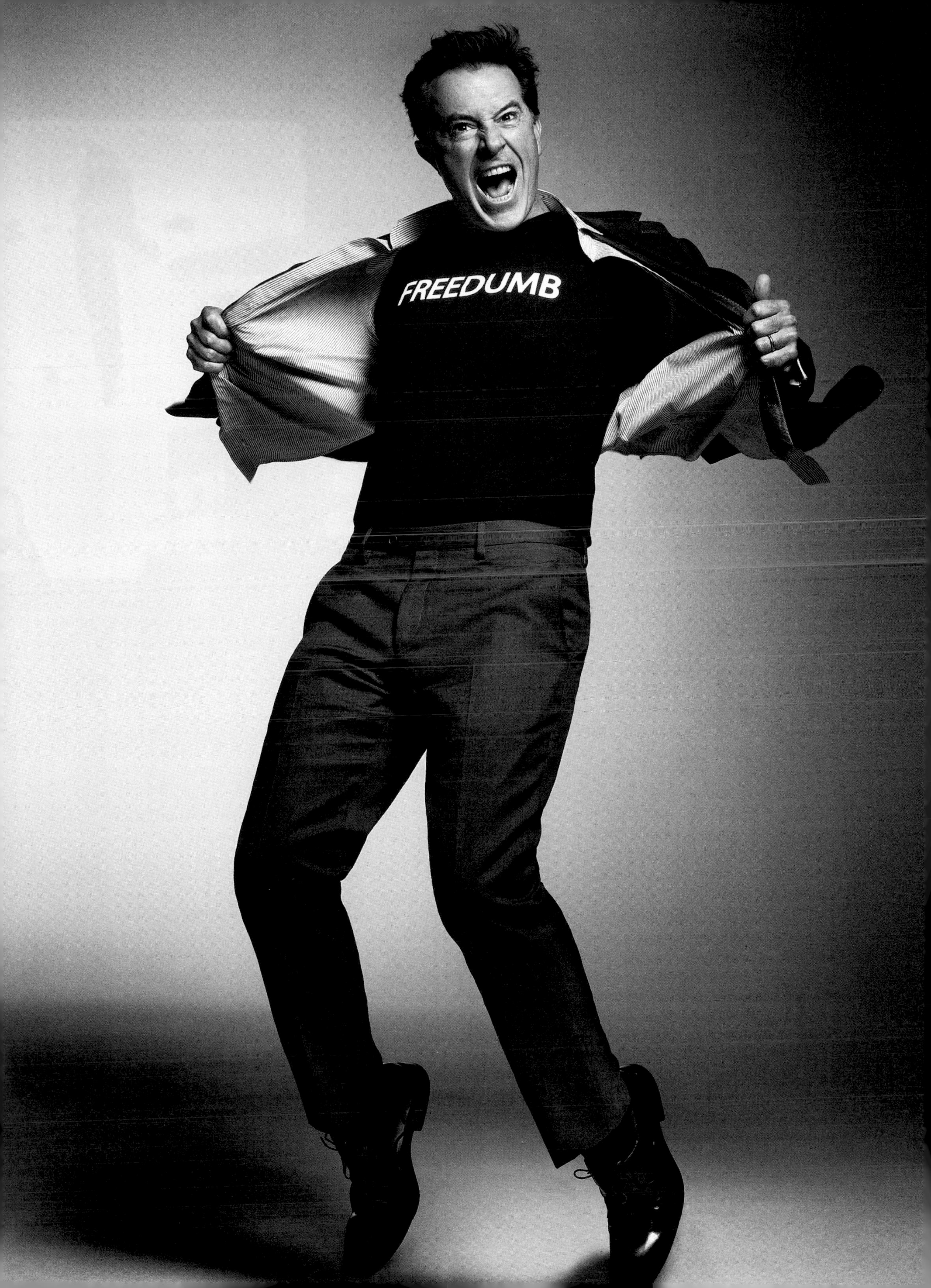
FREEDUMB

movie nor even in a dead-on comedy sketch. The new era required a new format. Colbert's medium, his sculptor's stone, would be himself. His masterwork, an extended, fully in-character piece of performance art, has run for eight years and counting.

On Oct. 17, 2005, *The Colbert Report* debuted, its host waving an American flag over the opening titles as a bald eagle flew straight at the camera and hortatory adjectives scrolled past ("BOLD . . . VALIANT . . . HELL-BENT"). In one of the show's first segments, Colbert introduced a word, "truthiness," that is more than a clever catchphrase; it is a 10-letter snapshot of the zeitgeist, capturing the idea that if something feels true, then it is. And if the "word police" at Webster's wouldn't sanction it (in fact, they named it 2006's Word of the Year), that only confirmed just how elitist factual knowledge was. "Who's *Britannica* to tell me the Panama Canal was finished in 1914?" Colbert asked. "If I want to say it happened in 1941, that's my right." America, he added, was divided between "those who think with their head and those who know with their heart."

Stephen Colbert may not be what most people conjure when they think of an artist. But in retrospect, that first episode was no less transformative than, say, the 1913 Armory Show. Like that breakthrough into modernism, *The Colbert Report* reframed our reality;

the world looked one way before it and another way after. A kind of mania, the anti-intellectual entitlement that had become the norm in public discourse, was suddenly revealed beneath the black light of Colbert's language and blustery, arch nerd swagger. He wasn't just performing his critique; he was becoming it.

And he was just getting started.

AT HEART, COLBERT'S PERFORMANCE DOES WHAT artistic genius throughout history has done: it takes something personal, essential to its creator, and finds a way to connect it to the universal. Stephen Colbert was not necessarily born to play "Stephen Colbert," but in a very real way he grew into the role.

Starting with his voice. As Colbert told NPR's Terry Gross in a 2005 interview, he adopted a kind of TV-anchor persona when he was just a kid in Charleston, S.C. "I grew up in the South, but I don't have a Southern accent," he said. "Not because I don't like Southern accents—I'm actually sort of sad that I don't have a Southern accent—but as a kid, I'd look at TV, and I would see that people with Southern accents were portrayed as being stupid. . . . I remember thinking, Oh, I kind of want to talk like John Chancellor. I want to talk like Cronkite. I want to talk like newspeople, because they seem smart and high-status, and what could be better than that?"

**FACING THE NATION**
*Since his days on
The Daily Show,
Colbert has continued
to call out the powers
that be from his studio
and the campaign trail.*

Colbert's name itself is also a conscious act of presentation. His parents gave him and his 10 siblings the choice of pronouncing their surname "KOHL-bert" or "kohl-BEAR"; Stephen started to use the francophone variation when he headed off to college. (Some of his siblings—like sister Elizabeth Colbert-Busch, who recently ran unsuccessfully for Congress in her home state—went the Americanized route.)

This focus on self-presentation and self-invention may help to explain why, as an acting student at Northwestern University, Colbert moved from an interest in drama to improv, performing with the Annoyance Theatre and Second City. (Tellingly, even as a young actor, he'd stay up until 4 a.m. after gigs, watching the late news.) He eventually moved to New York, where he worked stints writing for *Saturday Night Live* and *The Dana Carvey Show,* then landed the job that allowed him to begin to develop the character that would become his professional life.

It took some time for Colbert to become "Colbert." Unlike a novel or a painting, a comedy character goes through its rough drafts and revisions before the public's eyes. On Craig Kilborn's version of *The Daily Show,* Colbert's roving correspondent was a more generic than political idiot. But even in those early manifestations, you could see him working toward something beyond the standard handsome-guy caricature. What he was portraying was an insecure man with more status than talent, who high-handedly bluffed his way through stand-ups and interviews like some exotic frilled lizard inflating in self-defense. He could never drop the ostentation lest he reveal how small he really was. No blandly dull news guy, he stood at the intersection of status and fear.

When Jon Stewart took over *The Daily Show,* he encouraged Colbert to inject a more specific point of view into his characterization, and soon TV Colbert was moving closer to the heightened know-nothing conservatism we recognize today. (Though Colbert has described himself as liberal, he says he didn't really discover an interest in political commentary until working with Stewart.) Eventually, *The Daily Show* work spurred talk of a spin-off, and with it a realization that the new show would require more than a character at its center; it would need an idea.

The idea: we find ourselves immersed in a political media culture in which passion trumps fact, loyalty trumps reason, and personal brand trumps all, a polarized environment in which partisans assume bad faith on the part of anyone who disagrees with them.

47

Colbert modeled his show on cable news dojos like *The O'Reilly Factor,* which have succeeded by reinforcing an audience's worldview night after night—confirmation bias as programming strategy. *The Colbert Report's* satire is unmistakably political, setting up its host as a papa-bear reactionary like those who dominate the ratings over at Fox News.

But "Stephen Colbert" is only partly a satire of conservatives; above all he is a satire of idiots, of a culture that sneers at science and "elitist" learning. The Stephen Colbert of *The Daily Show* was a journalist who rose through the ranks despite his ignorance, because he did his best to hide it; the host of *The Colbert Report* is successful *because* he is ignorant— and proud of it. "That, I think, is the nutmeat of the show," he said in a 2005 interview with TIME. "Enough mind. We tried mind for a long time, and what has it gotten us? You know, except for vaccinations."

The fake Colbert is an ingenious, nimble performance, a peacock with two right wings, goading the audience—his "Nation"—to cheer him wildly as he debates himself in a segment called "Formidable Opponent," or bloviating through tortured rationalizations of the Iraq War. The character uses Colbert's talent for aping mannerisms of authority: the alpha-anchor baritone, the flagpole posture, the cocked eyebrow.

His interviews are delicate tap dances fueled by his long-practiced improv skills. He lets his guests make their points against the backdrop of his bluster, but he also lets the quick wit of his real self peek through the pancake makeup. Questioning astrophysicist Neil deGrasse Tyson about whether or not Pluto should be considered a planet, he argued, "Isn't that just East Coast liberal intellectuals—Ivy League–educated people—telling us what is or isn't a planet?"

OF COURSE, EACH COMPONENT OF THIS satire has been seen before. The innovation of *The Colbert Report* is in its scale. Each night, Colbert hosts, reads the news, offers editorials and does interviews—all in character, the same character. He's been doing it now for almost a decade; as a single, sustained performance, it easily surpasses any Andy Kaufman stunt. Nor can it be compared to a scripted comedy: although "Stephen Colbert" is a fake person (even if he shares some biography—Catholicism, South Carolina roots—with the actual version), he clearly interacts with the real world.

# DEFINING TALENTS
Even art has its rules—but every now and then someone comes along and rewrites them

### ❶ Matt Groening
#### CARTOONIST
In 1999, TIME dubbed *The Simpsons* the best TV show of the century, and Groening's disarmingly vile cartoon still delivers the ultimate takedown of the American family. Should you disagree, our shorts are available for your dining pleasure.

### ❷ Meryl Streep
#### ACTRESS
With three Oscars, 17 nominations, some of the most iconic roles ever—in *The Deer Hunter, Sophie's Choice, Kramer vs. Kramer* and *The Iron Lady*—and all those spot-on accents, she is one of the most accomplished performers of our time.

### ❸ Frank Gehry
#### ARCHITECT
Wavelike surfaces that shimmer and change shape with the light. Undulating forms inspired by the flitting carp his grandmother kept. This is architecture as art. Starchitect? More like superstarchitect.

### ❹ Prince
#### MUSICIAN
Eclectic, daring, sometimes infuriating, always visionary—few musical artists combine diverse genres with such effortless success and prodigious playing. Plus, he practically trademarked flat-out bad-boy sexy.

This, of course, gives Colbert a stage much bigger than the one in his studio, and it means his performance can extend well beyond his 11:30-to-midnight slot. In April 2006, Colbert was the featured entertainer at the White House Correspondents Association dinner in Washington, D.C. He roasted President Bush, who was sitting just chairs away: "He stands for things. Not only *for* things, he stands *on* things. Things like aircraft carriers and rubble and recently flooded city squares." He also took down, brutally, the press corps that filled the room. "Over the last five years you people were so good," Colbert said, "over tax cuts, WMD intelligence, the effect of global warming. We Americans didn't want to know, and you had the courtesy not to try to find out."

After the event, journalists said his routine wasn't funny, but to the audience outside the room who watched by the millions on YouTube, it felt like a fever breaking after five years of acquiescent post-9/11 reporting. Colbert had figured out how to turn a late-night comedy shtick into something like a movement. Just as the pundits who were his targets had become brands that extended beyond their shows—into books, appearances, national rallies—he had extended his brand, too, and in so doing, sent up both politics and that branding in one metaguerrilla act. To parody an age of egomaniacs and their brands, he branded himself an egomaniac.

Colbert ran a favorite-son campaign in the 2008 South Carolina primary—convincing Doritos to sponsor him—which then became a vehicle to educate his viewers about the campaign-finance system. He urged

## 'COLBERT' IS FAKE, BUT HE INTERACTS WITH THE REAL WORLD.

Nation members to edit Wikipedia entries to substantiate his false claims, thus putting into practice another of his pet coinages, "Wikiality," the notion that truth has become a manipulatable construct. And he lobbied to get his name on a Hungarian bridge (voters said yes, officials said no), a Ben & Jerry's flavor (AmeriCone Dream) and a room on the International Space Station (he settled for a treadmill).

Maybe Colbert's greatest act of entangling art-

istry with reality was his move in 2011 to establish a Super PAC—an independent political action committee with unlimited fundraising potential. To show how this new kind of spending group, legitimized by the Supreme Court's Citizens United ruling, gave the wealthy outsized influence, Colbert, in typically egotistical character, asked his fans to donate money to underwrite his own outsized individual influence.

Colbert's show was soon a nightly tutorial in the buying of democracy. He invited Trevor Potter, former chairman of the Federal Election Commission, to walk him through the process of filing. ("What's a Super PAC? Is that a PAC that got bitten by a radioactive lobbyist?") Then he explained gleefully that the PAC, which once would have been considered an illegal "in-kind contribution" from his corporate employer Viacom, was now 100% legal. Colbert raised over a million dollars, with which he bought a series of wildly negative attack ads, and he never tired of pointing out that no one was obligated to reveal who had funded them. When he toyed with another congressional run in South Carolina, he signed over control of his Super PAC to Stewart, who definitely—wink, wink!—would "not coordinate" with his Comedy Central colleague, just as political Super PACs were never in contact—wink, wink!—with their favored candidates.

It was, in other words, a classic work of postmodernism, cutting through—like a Philip Roth novel or Cindy Sherman photograph—the distinction between creator and character, fiction and reality and, in this case, political satire and actual political activity.

Not to be lost in the performance was the fact that it was all to make a deadly important point. "Some people have cynically asked: Is this some kind of joke?" Colbert said at a press conference after filing his papers. "I, for one, don't think that participating in democracy is a joke. I don't think that wanting to know what the rules are is a joke. But I do have one federal-election-law joke, if you'd like to hear it: Knock, knock. [*Who's there?*] Unlimited union and corporate campaign contributions. [*Unlimited union and corporate campaign contributions who?*] That's the thing, I don't think I should have to tell you."

Was it serious? Yes. Was it funny? Hilarious. But was it a joke? That was and continues to be for us to decide. Trusting his fans' intelligence, their willingness to engage with ideas, and their belief that—whatever his character says—truth does indeed matter more than truthiness . . . that is, sadly, what makes Stephen Colbert unique.

### 5 Rei Kawakubo
**FASHION DESIGNER**

She refuses to characterize the unconstructed, otherworldly clothing she designs as art, but we will. Since she launched Comme des Garçons in 1973, Kawakubo has never ceased to amaze and enthrall—and dress us as no one else dares.

### 6 Gerhard Richter
**ARTIST**

Crossing and recrossing borders as he blurs the lines between painting, photography and sculpture—not to mention the real, surreal and unreal—the protean, prolific German is among the preeminent visual creators of the past half-century.

### 7 Julie Taymor
**THEATER DIRECTOR**

From film to opera to the magical realm of *The Lion King* (her best-director Tony was a first for a woman on Broadway), Taymor spreads her multimedia vision like a spider(man)'s web to prove just how dramatic drama can be.

### 8 Junot Diaz
**WRITER**

From the hell of Trujillo's Dominican Republic to the uncertainties of life in the U.S., Diaz's antic novels and stories chronicle a world of broken hearts and divided loyalties. Diaz writes about Dominican Americans, but he tells the story of all America.

# HEY, LOOK AT ME!

BY BELINDA LUSCOMBE

*Sure, everyone can be famous for 15 minutes. The charismatic genius knows how to make it last*

Any reasonably cogent human with a full set of limbs (and even that may set the bar too high) can become a star. No particular talent is required, merely luck and drive and the eye-wateringly hard work of a few dedicated handlers. That's one hypothesis, and it seems to be promoted at times even by famous folk themselves. Didn't Lady Gaga sing, "My mamma told me when I was young we're all born superstars"? The other theory is this: stars are a breed apart, freaks of nature who possess something out of the ordinary, something that makes them more luminous and twinkly and volcanic than the rest of us. Most of the proponents of the former view are academics or journalists who ponder stardom from afar or chronicle the business of celebrity. Champions of the latter view tend to be people who actually know a superstar or two. Or are their agents.

As a man in charge of finding young talent, Gary Marsh, now president and chief creative officer of Disney Channels Worldwide, has guided several young hopefuls along the road from obscurity to international fame. Disney, in fact, had quite a production line going there for a while, churning out the likes of Miley Cyrus, the Jonas Brothers and Demi Lovato, young entertainers who started with TV shows, then moved on to record

**STAR POWER** *Actress Selena Gomez (far left), pro quarterback Tim Tebow (center), and the fowl-hunting Robertsons of* Duck Dynasty *may not be the most talented at what they do. But they have what it takes to be famous.*

music, design clothing lines and grace lunch boxes. By the time they were through, they had become monarchs of genuine multimedia empires. But that transformation is no given. In an interview with Time in 2009, Marsh claimed that, though stars can be nurtured, they cannot be manufactured. Stars are different.

When he needed a Latina teen for a new show his employer was planning a few years back, Marsh went on a cross-country tour, throwing his star-catching net as wide as possible. Thousands of parents brought him their daughters to see if they might fit the glass slipper he was offering. But every hopeful fell short—except for a single spunky preteen by the name of Selena Gomez. "She was the only one," Marsh said.

His proposition, that fame isn't just a product of happenstance or smoke and mirrors, is seconded by an unlikely source. Jeffrey Sachs, the noted economist who is director of the Earth Institute, has worked with several stars in their roles as "celanthropists," famous men and women who want to turn the limelight that always follows them toward some of the darker corners of our planet. Stars, Sachs says, have a particular gift, or a combination of gifts, that enables them to break through the populist hubbub. "In the very noisy and complicated

world that we have, people that reach large numbers of people, like Madonna does, have an extraordinarily important role to play," he has said.

Of course, celebrity has become contested ground of late. The tsunami of reality TV has washed dozens of new arrivals up on the shores of Fameland. And just when it seemed as if the beachhead could take no more, social media bloomed, and suddenly anyone could be famous—a kid whose dental anesthesia hadn't worn off, another whose brother bit his finger, a grumpy cat.

But in the end, that is chance fame, not the kind that draws people to part with their money or time or dreamy moments. Here's a handy litmus test to establish star cred: Do you care more about who they are than what they do? Will Smith's geniality has brought people to many a mediocre movie. *After Earth* was his first box-office bomb in two decades. Not even technically great actors like Meryl Streep can pull that off. People watch football just to see Tim Tebow play, despite the fact that he's a pretty inconsistent quarterback. There are about 2½ million waterfowl hunters in the U.S., and yet more than three times that number tune in to see what Phil Robertson and his clan are up to every week on *Duck Dynasty.* Angelina Jolie hasn't

had a hit movie in eight years (2005's *Mr. & Mrs. Smith*), but her announcement about undergoing a preventive double mastectomy pushed breast cancer onto front pages everywhere.

What do Tebow and Jolie, Smith and the Robertson crew have in common? The ability to grab and hold our attention. These days it's not hard to catch the public's eye; one good YouTube video or heinous crime will do it. But holding that attention is another matter. To stay famous, stars need a lens-clear picture not just of what the public wants in general, but what they want from the fame chaser in particular and how much of it they can stand. The wrong movie or tweet, too much silence or too many appearances, an inappropriate outfit or an inopportune photo—any of these can be ruinous. Self-promotion is the art of rocking the boat as wildly as possible without tipping it over.

Yes, famous people have teams offering them counsel on what to do and whom to avoid, how they are perceived and how to enhance or change that perception. But the real celebrity masterminds seem to have an innate sense of it all. When asked if she ever got tired of always being so outrageous, Lady Gaga answered that it would be unsustainable if she weren't really, at least a little, like that.

It would also be unsustainable if she didn't actually want all the attention. When fame does come, it brings with it a share of burdens, more than enough to force many to opt out after their first couple of laps around the track. Natural celebrities have a hunger for the hunger. They need to know that others need to know about them. They draw life force from flashbulbs and headlines and Web searches.

Take the simple act of choosing a child's name.

**BRIGHT LIGHTS** *Will Smith (top left), Angelina Jolie (bottom left), Lady Gaga (center), and Kanye West and Kim Kardashian (above) are the embodiment of A-list celebrity, boasting an ability to grab and hold our attention while drawing life force from flashbulbs and headlines.*

It was probably inevitable that West, a hip-hop superstar whose name is recognized by—conservatively—a gajillion times more people than those who can sing any of his songs, would end up with Kardashian, a woman whose entire professional life has been devoted to making herself unavoidable. The name of their unborn daughter was the subject of much discussion; the pressure to present something suitably buzzworthy, while not too ornate or obvious, was heavy. Nevertheless, the duo managed to flabbergast an already very jaded public by calling their daughter North. The ingenuity of this name cannot be overstated: it's simple, staggeringly inappropriate with that surname—and unforgettable. Game, set and match to little North West's parents.

How did they hit upon something so exquisitely honed to cause the most astonishment? Who knows? The specialness of math whizzes and piano prodigies is obvious, but what makes a celebrity a celebrity isn't easy to pinpoint. And it's unlikely that science will isolate the chromosomes where the self-promotion gene lies anytime soon.

Maybe that kind of genius isn't one talent but a strange combination of skills, including single-mindedness, an insensitivity to other pleasures and the ability to ruthlessly prioritize. Then again, lots of successful people have those. What sets apart the self-promotional elite is their knack for projecting an enormous comfort with who they are and for getting us to feel that comfort too. George Clooney, Tom Hanks, Henry Kissinger, Hillary Clinton and, yes, Phil Robertson—they all make us believe that their charm is reliable, that their charisma will never run dry, and that ultimately, resistance to their magnetism is futile. It's not overconfidence so much as well-founded confidence, and it becomes a self-fulfilling prophecy.

An incandescent belief in the self—on top of that atypical mix of ability, charisma, vision, adaptability and optimism it takes to become really famous—is its own form of genius. Thank goodness there's no Nobel Prize awarded for it. The winners would be impossible.

For almost every parent, it has special significance. Whether they're named after a saint or a grandmother or a personal hero, sons and daughters carry the stamp of their parents' values and personalities for the rest of their days. No surprise, then, that the bigger the celebrity, the more finely calibrated their offspring's name will be to attract notice.

The history books haven't settled on the Typhoid Mary of headline-grabbing baby names, but '60s musician Frank Zappa, with Dweezil and Moon Unit, or '80s rock star Bob Geldof with Fifi Trixibelle, Peaches and Pixie were certainly watershed figures in the movement. Once the press signed onto this particular celebrity affectation, a positive feedback cycle, not to mention Apple Martin, was born.

The cycle recently reached perfect-storm proportions when Kanye West sired a child with Kim Kardashian.

# THE ART OF MORE

BY GARY BELSKY

*To find a financial genius you have to look beyond the biggest bank account*

L IKE "NERVOUS BREAKDOWN," PHRASES LIKE "BUSINESS GENIUS" OR "FINANCIAL GENIUS" DON'T mean much once you start to drill down a bit. They are layman's terms that signify at once nothing and everything about a subject of great nuance and variety. What does it mean, after all, to be a genius when it comes to money? Was Adam Smith, the 18th-century Scottish philosopher, a genius because of his insights into how economies work? Does Mexican industrialist Carlos Slim qualify because, with an estimated fortune upward of $70 billion, he's one of the richest men on the planet? How about Thomas Edison, who, by inventing the lightbulb, phonograph and movie camera, almost single-handedly created three entire industries from scratch?

"It gets down to the fundamental question posed by the 'great person' versus 'zeitgeist' theories of history," says University of California, Davis, professor of psychology Dean Keith Simonton, a leading expert on genius. "Is this person a genuine 'genius,' or did he/she just happen to be at the right place at the right time?" Simonton points out that we assign different weight to these questions depending on which area of achievement is under discussion—art, say, versus science or politics. "It is obvious that Michelangelo was a genius," Simonton says. "The Sistine Chapel would look very different today otherwise. Yet when we get to economic history, the picture becomes more clouded by situational factors. If Andrew Carnegie had never come to the U.S., would the heavy-steel industry not have developed here? Of course not!"

**ORACLE OF OMAHA**
*Warren Buffett, the third-richest man on the planet, always sticks to his own convictions, whatever other investors may do.*

In 1790, the German philosopher Immanuel Kant famously described genius as "the talent for producing that for which no definite rule can be

**MONEY TALKS** *Do all his diversified holdings make Carlos Slim a genius? Maybe not, but they do make him very rich.*

given," adding that for any thought or act to even be considered genius, it has to be both original and exemplary. "By 'original,'" explains Simonton, "we mean that nobody else in the same field had come up with the same idea. And by 'exemplary,' we mean that the idea is not just useful but worthy of admiration, even imitation."

What does this definition tell us about the people in business, economics and finance today who are most often pegged as geniuses? Plenty of information-technology firms, to consider one example, have imitated many of Michael Bloomberg's innovations at his eponymous data and media company. (Exemplary? Check.) Then again, the Bloomberg Terminal was far from the first such device on Wall Street. (Original? No.) So is New York City's mayor a genius or just a smart businessman? And what about Yale economist Robert Shiller, who correctly identified the price bubbles in both technology stocks and U.S. real estate in the past decade and a half? Do his insights earn him hallowed status? That, too, depends on your criteria. Explains Emanuel Derman, head of Columbia University's graduate financial-engineering program and the author of *Models Behaving Badly*, "There's a difference between thinking about money and making money."

Indeed, to decide what it means to be a genius in matters of money, we need first to understand three different kinds of exemplary and original thinking—and thinkers—that have inspired the description.

## ECONOMIC GENIUS.

Any investigation into financial genius will surely turn up a handful of individuals who have won—or would have won, had they lived long enough—a Nobel Prize in Economic Sciences. As it happens, experts on the production, distribution and consumption of goods, services and wealth are currently enjoying a rare moment in the spotlight, even if most of those attention-drawing economists are dead. This is in large part thanks to a heated debate over the role of government in jump-starting and maintaining economic growth, which pits devotees of John Maynard Keynes (1883-1946), who favor intervention, against those of Friedrich Hayek (1899-1992) and Milton Friedman (1912-2006), who were more skeptical about such centralized efforts. All three men were brilliant and original thinkers, but economics is in many ways an incremental science: Economists are essentially scholarly tweakers who synthesize their thinking with the work of others into new analyses and theories. Even Adam Smith, who is considered no less than the father of economics, built his famous concept about the "invisible hand" that guides markets atop previous work by the Irish economist Richard Cantillon.

At the same time, some of the most original

Nobel-worthy work in economics has as much to do with math as money. Take, for instance, notable big thinkers like Fischer Black, Myron Scholes and Robert Merton, who in the 1970s created a formula for pricing certain kinds of securities; or William Sharpe, who in the 1960s helped to devise a way to analyze investment performance that accounts for the amount of risk taken. These men spent their academic and/or business careers in finance, but their achievements were in the realm of applied mathematics; finance just happened to be the field in which they were applied. Had they decided to help NASA send men into space rather than help investors get richer, they might well have ended up on a list of scientific geniuses.

"I'm not sure there are many true economic geniuses alive right now," says the economist Russell Roberts, a research fellow at Stanford's Hoover Institute and host of the popular EconTalk podcast. Roberts thinks University of Chicago professor Gary Becker, with whom he studied, may be the rare one, for his Nobel winning use of economic theory to understand all sorts of human behaviors, from race relations to crime to drug addiction. "He applied economics to everything else before it was fashionable," says Roberts.

### ENTREPRENEURIAL GENIUS.

Economics is at heart the study of resource allocation: how individuals and institutions utilize the materials, time, labor and ideas within their reach. It's a messy business—literally and figuratively—which is why those who figure out how to do it usually end up with a pile of cash and, every once in a while, the designation of genius. Titans like Walmart founder Sam Walton, McDonald's boss Ray Kroc or automaker Henry Ford may not have invented (respectively) discount retailing, fast food or the car business, but each gave new order to existing resources and in so doing changed popular culture. "Henry Ford's genius was in organization," says Philip Lawton of Research Affiliates, a research investment-management firm in Newport Beach, Calif. "He put labor, technology and materials together in a way no one had before." Ford, in other words, had vision. He saw paths through forests where others only saw trees.

The same is true of Microsoft cofounder Bill Gates and Virgin Atlantic impresario Richard Branson, multi-media icon Oprah Winfrey and Amazon founder Jeff Bezos. While all could be described to greater or lesser extent as innovators, what each clearly represents is the successful marshaling of vision, drive and resources into transformative businesses. This is

entrepreneurial genius at work, says Simonton, reflecting "high general intelligence, mastery of a field, openness to experience, risk-taking willingness and extremely high motivation—persistence and energy—to surmount whatever obstacles may get in the way." That last bit tellingly hearkens back to Edison's definition of genius as "1% inspiration and 99% perspiration." Whether on a focused mission or just hacking away aimlessly, forging paths through the woods is hard work. Sam Walton was 44 when he opened the first Walmart and already a veteran of more than two decades in retailing. "Financial genius is finding the flaws in a market and exploiting them," says bestselling author Michael Lewis, whose book *The Big Short* dissected the 2008 mortgage crisis. "It's mostly about having a talent for business and combining it with a lot of hard work."

### INVESTMENT GENIUS.

In no other financial arena is the term "genius" thrown around with more abandon and less justification than on Wall Street, where any money manager on a sustained hot streak is likely to earn the label. But however long an investor outperforms the market, there will almost always be a subsequent reversion to the mean—a falling back to the less successful crowd—and that suggests that randomness plays a disproportionate and hard-to-measure role in performance. "There's nobody I can think of who I'm certain is an investment genius," says University of Chicago behavioral economist Richard Thaler. "It's still really hard to sort the skillful from the lucky." This appraisal has been confirmed in countless academic studies that show that above-average investment performance is both unpredictable and unsustainable. Set enough people to the task of picking stocks, bonds,

**TREND SETTER** *University of Chicago professor Gary Becker was the first to apply economics to social issues such as racial discrimination in the workplace.*

# 'INVESTING IS MOST INTELLIGENT WHEN IT IS MOST BUSINESSLIKE. CALL IT HAVING INDEPENDENCE OF MIND.'

**MOVERS AND MAKERS**
*(clockwise from top left): Proving there are many different ways to cash in, Virgin Group founder Richard Branson traded as much on his personality as on his business sense. Entrepreneur Jeff Bezos—the man behind Amazon.com, the world's largest online retailer—focused on the long view. And Oprah Winfrey developed a committed TV fan base before starting a magazine and a network.*

best book ever written on investing."

Graham believed that the key to stock picking was an understanding that each share of a company is something more than a bet on price; rather, it is an ownership stake in an actual business. That this insight is obvious should not detract from its brilliance. Every rapid change in a company's share price—in any asset price, for that matter—is another grain of proof that many if not most investors fail to grasp Graham's lesson. After all, how could the knowable value of entities as vast and complex as, say, General Motors or Google change as often as their securities' prices do?

Graham's genius was his willingness to ignore such short-term signals to focus on deeper measures of value. The same is true of Buffett. "The quality I think of when considering the genius of Graham or Buffett is actually more about character than intelligence," says *Wall Street Journal* columnist Jason Zweig, who edited and provided commentary for a 2006 update of *The Intelligent Investor*. "Graham said investing is most intelligent when it is most businesslike. I would call it having independence of mind."

Buffett, in other words, has been as successful as he has been not only because he understands Graham's principles but because he sticks to them no matter what other investors are doing. And despite an estimated fortune of $59 billion—the third-largest on the planet—Buffett knows that wads of cash alone are no measure of genius (case in point: Donald Trump). "It's not a numerical value that matters," says NYU finance professor Nassim Taleb, author of the bestselling *Antifragile: Things That Gain from Disorder*. "It's not even what you know about making money that matters. It's how you express it in a way that doesn't harm you when you're wrong."

Here's what Taleb means: in a typical Berkshire Hathaway annual report, Buffett invariably spends a few pages of his letter to shareholders detailing the company's core operations, insurance. But he's especially clear about one aspect of the business: risk. In 2012, he wrote that "we are far more conservative in avoiding risk than most large companies. For example, if the insurance industry should experience a $250 billion loss from some megacatastrophe—a loss about triple anything it has ever experienced—Berkshire as a whole would likely record a significant profit for the year because it has so many streams of earnings."

Although he was not explicitly discussing the makeup of financial genius, Buffett revealed that he well understands the most basic precept of its nature: make the most, while risking the least.

real estate, precious metals or corn futures, and over time, a handful will turn out to be enormously successful at it. The same would be true whether all of them were George Soros, who is considered one of the smartest money managers in history, or Homer Simpson, who is not.

In fact, the book often called the bible of professional investors, *Security Analysis,* was coauthored nearly 80 years ago by a man who believed that too much of what passed for investing was actually speculation—that is, gambling. His name was Benjamin Graham, a Columbia University professor and private money manager who owes much of his ongoing cultural relevance to the identity of one his students: Warren Buffett, a.k.a. the Oracle of Omaha, who garners the most votes among amateurs and experts alike as a reigning financial genius. The chairman of Berkshire Hathaway would dismiss such a description for himself, but he might allow it for his mentor, whose 1949 book for a more general audience, *The Intelligent Investor,* Buffett describes as "by far the

# A HIGHER POWER

BY SEAN GREGORY

*LeBron James is fit and fast, but it's athletic genius that allows him to do on the court what others can't*

LeBron James's computer—the potent one inside his head—has picked up on something: Udonis Haslem is hot. Watching Haslem shoot a basketball is not unlike sitting through a nude scene on Netflix with your folks. His shot is ugly, herky-jerky; it makes you cringe. But here, in the third quarter of Game 4 of the Miami Heat's opening-round playoff series with the Milwaukee Bucks, he has hit three in a row.

James catches a pass at the top of the key and takes two dribbles to his left. Three defenders surround him. Haslem is hanging out in the right corner, but his matchup, Bucks center Larry Sanders, is cheating toward the middle to offer still more help on James.

Not that it makes a difference. As James plows through the first three Bucks, Sanders fully commits to stopping the 6'8", 250-pound locomotive, who continues to pick up speed. James leaps above him, on his way, it seems, taking a left-handed layup. Now a fifth defender, the backboard, hovers over James as well. It can't stop him either.

**UNTOUCHABLE** *LeBron James, seen here grabbing one of 10 rebounds in Game 6 of the 2013 NBA Finals, has led the Miami Heat to back-to-back championships.*

In the air, James makes a split-second decision and flicks a pass to an open Haslem. Because LeBron James—like Magic Johnson and Larry Bird before him—sees what others cannot. He reads the geometry of the game and spots openings before everyone else does. Of course, that wouldn't matter if he didn't also have the physical aptitude to deliver what his brain commands. James's pass is simple and subtle. But to a discerning eye it is more beautiful and thrilling than one of his monstrous dunks or circus moves that regularly light up *SportsCenter.* Haslem sinks the shot.

Before the game is over, James dishes out four more clever assists, like a Vegas card dealer. A cross-court fastball to Ray Allen for a corner three-pointer. An open shot for Mario Chalmers, as James, jumping forward, somehow spots his teammate behind him, changes direction in flight, and *bam.* Then there's one dribble and—*flick*—a shovel pass to Shane Battier, for another three. And finally, as Milwaukee's Monta Ellis leaves Allen to help cover Chalmers as he cuts to the basket, *whooosh,* a 100 m.p.h. strike right in Allen's chest, for one more uncontested three. James finishes with 30 points, 8 rebounds and 7 assists. Miami wins the game and the series.

Yes, LeBron James is LeBron James because he's a chiseled and oversized specimen who is also freakishly fast and coordinated enough to have mastered at the highest level the fundamental skills of basketball: dribbling, shooting and passing. But he is a once-in-a-generation talent because he can also so easily process multiple bits of information in real time. *Where's my defender? Where's my teammate's defender? Should I go left or right—and what will each open up in the defense?* To paraphrase another physical genius, hockey icon Wayne Gretzky, a good player knows where

# MASTERS OF THE GAMES
## Some other athletes gifted beyond compare
### BY MICHAEL NEILL

**PEYTON MANNING**
He made the Indianapolis Colts an NFL power, taking them to the Super Bowl twice, with an instantaneous—and laser-sharp—reading of defenses that redefined the job of quarterback.

**LIONEL MESSI**
Barcelona's scoring machine is the brightest fútbol star on the planet—and one of the best ever—because, says a former manager, he is the only player who "runs faster with the ball than without it."

**SERENA WILLIAMS**
At 31, the 2013 French Open champion is once again the world's top women's tennis player. Her athleticism—see that eye-popping physique—overpowers opponents; her rocket-powered serve demolishes them.

the ball is. A great player knows where it is going to be.

What separates James—and Gretzky and the vanishingly rare others like them in other sports—from the more mortal competition is that he has conditioned his body to make the right move at the right time way more often than anyone else. Elite athletes call on their own brand of genius every game, against a host of others focused on ensuring their failure. That mathematician scripting a groundbreaking proof? How would he do with four 300-pound linemen chasing him around his office?

"Sports offer some unfathomable thing that is beyond scientific explanation," says Jacob Soll, a history professor at the University of Southern California who won a MacArthur Foundation "genius grant" in 2011 for his research on early modern Europe. "Athletes make moves that are beautiful, not logical, but work. In the best moments, they do things that make you go, 'Oh my god, that's amazing.' Is there genius in sports? Yes."

The late author David Foster Wallace, another MacArthur Fellow, used the word "genius" 16 times in his 1994 essay about tennis star Tracy Austin, a former teenage prodigy. "Top athletes are profound," Foster Wallace wrote, "because they make a certain kind of genius as carnally discernible as it ever can get." To Wallace, top jocks were "beautiful: Jordan hanging in midair like a Chagall bride, Sampras laying down a touch volley at an angle that defies Euclid. And they're inspiring. There is about world-class athletes carving out exemptions from physical laws a transcendent beauty that makes manifest God in man ... Great athletes are profundity in motion. They enable abstractions like *power* and *grace* and *control* to become not only incarnate but televisable. To be a top athlete, performing, is to be that exquisite hybrid of animal and ing the location of a 130 m.p.h. serve or trying to thread a pass between two lightning-quick defensive backs. Still, would pro athletes benefit from an occasional electrical injection to the brain? "We can't say for sure," says Celnik. "But the implication is there. And that's exciting and cool."

JAMES NEEDS NO ELECTRODES. IN 2013 his team won its second straight championship, and he earned his fourth regular-season MVP award. Only four others—Kareem Abdul-Jabbar, Michael Jordan, Wilt Chamberlain and Bill Russell, Hall of Famers all—have won as many. "He's brilliant, really," says Duke's Mike Krzyzewski, who coached James in the 2008 and 2012 Olympics, both gold-medal wins for the USA. "I can go through, say, five sets that Spain runs, on a chalkboard or on tape. When we go to the court and start walking through trying to learn it in real time, he already knows them. And not only does he know them, he has already thought about his reactionary moves to their movement."

Part of James's brilliance is self-taught and hard-won, the result of his particular mix of singular talent and single-minded commitment. In 2011, as Miami was losing the NBA finals to the Dallas Mavericks, a flaw in James's game was revealed: a propensity to hang around the perimeter, 20 feet from the basket. With the physical advantage he holds over most every foe, that tactic was a huge waste of resources. If he had camped much closer to the hoop, he could have overpowered or outmaneuvered the defense to get a higher percentage of shots. Watching James in that series was like watching someone chuck diamonds into the sea.

James saw it too. He visited former Houston Rockets center Hakeem Olajuwon, a Hall of Famer known as a Baryshnikov around the basket.

**TIGER WOODS**
Playing with eerie consistency, he has won more majors than any player in recent history. A big hitter with a delicate touch for the short game, he is also an unflappable master of the mental game.

**MIGUEL CABRERA**
A pure swing like this comes along once in a baseball generation, which may explain why, in 2012, he became the first player in 45 years to achieve the Triple Crown. The Detroit Tigers' 29-year-old All-Star third baseman is simply the best hitter in the game— and he's only getting better.

**FLOYD MAYWEATHER JR.**
The five-star ring general is a master boxer who flashes deadly hand speed, punishing power and unparalleled defensive skills. It all adds up to an undefeated welterweight/ superwelterweight champ— and the richest athlete in the world.

Olajuwon's footwork led the Rockets to back-to-back titles in 1994 and 1995. He says, "I'd get to the gym a little early, but he was already ready to go. He really wanted to get better."

In the area of the court known as the low post, basketball is a chess match, as the offensive player reacts to what a defender gives him or tries to create space to operate. "You make a move to get the defense to shift weight, say, to his right leg," says Olajuwon. "Then you attack that leg. He cannot move and you're gone."

"You're recognizing a pattern," continues Olajuwon. "It's a science and an art, the art of creativity." After a week, James left Houston with a sharper post game. There is a genius in being able to accomplish whatever you set out to do.

Today, James is a more efficient scorer because of his new skills. His old skills, though, remain intact. "From the foul line down, I used to think the three best passers I'd seen were Larry Bird, Rick Barry and Charles Barkley," says longtime NBA analyst Hubie Brown, a former coach. "This guy is better."

Through those two straight title runs, James's brilliance was constantly on display: in the spinning post moves and fall-away shots, in the smothering defense and no-look passes and crossover dribbles. But his work ethic has never wavered: he spent the summer of 2012 honing his jump shot, then hit a career-high 41% from the three-point line in the 2012–13 season and several crucial mid-range shots in game 7 of the finals against the San Antonio Spurs.

Now consider this: James is only 28 years old. He will be pushing the limits—of his game, the game of basketball, and maybe all games—for years to come. "If he stays healthy," says Brown, "he will probably go down as the greatest player ever." Because in the end, genius is eternal.

# BATTLE STARS

BY KELLY KNAUER

*Military genius* *makes sure the biggest guns don't always win*

GREAT THEORISTS OF WAR, LIKE THOSE OF PHYSICS, MAY make their breakthroughs by conducting what Albert Einstein called a "thought experiment," never muddying their boots on a battlefield. Witness the Prussian Carl Philipp Gottfried von Clausewitz, who taught us that "war is the continuation of politics by other means." But many others, from Alexander the Great and George Washington to Napoleon and George S. Patton, were just the opposite: frontline charismatics who inspired the affection of their men while demanding the most from them. Some military geniuses are virtuosos of deception, following Stonewall Jackson's prescription to "always mystify." Others are manipulators of topography and logistics, seeing opportunities where others see only barriers. Hannibal, the great general of Carthage, attacked Rome from an unexpected space—the other side of the Alps. Vo Nguyen Giap used the jungle as camouflage and tunnels as attack routes. Visionaries and theorists, charismatic leaders and masters of surprise—these Einsteins in uniform clearly earned their stars.

# ◀ Hannibal Barca

The great general who led Carthage against Rome in the Second Punic War (218–201 B.C.) was a visionary who stunned the growing Roman Empire by attacking it on an unexpected front, dealing its legions one of the most severe battlefield defeats in Roman history.

As the two great trading empires vied for the markets of the Mediterranean, Carthage prospered through its control of the southern coast of today's Spain. It was there that Hannibal learned his profession, fighting to subdue local tribes and succeeding his father and brother as the leader of the army in Hispania. In 218 B.C., this master of logistics launched one of history's most brilliant invasions, taking an army of some 40,000 troops (and several-score battle elephants imported from Africa) across the Pyrenees, the Alps and an assortment of major rivers to attack Rome via its "back door"—the natural mountain barriers where its generals least expected an assault.

Rome fell victim to a Punic panic as Hannibal marched his troops down the Italian peninsula, joined by the warriors of many indigenous tribes who, restless under Roman rule, rallied to his cry: "I have come not to make war on the Italians, but to aid the Italians against Rome."

Hannibal won significant victories at Trebia and Lake Tasimene in northern Italy, then bypassed the imperial city to threaten its great granaries at Cannae, south and east of Rome. There, on Aug. 2, 216 B.C., Carthage's 50,000 troops won a memorable victory against Rome's 86,000 troops as Hannibal pioneered a powerful tactic, the pincer movement. Placing his weakest troops in the center of his position and his best troops to either side, he led a carefully calibrated retreat in the center that led the Romans to think they had the upper hand. It was, of course, a trap: once the Romans had penetrated deep into the Carthaginian lines, the two flanks closed around them in what later generals would term a "double envelopment." In the slaughter that followed, Rome lost more than 50,000 soldiers—and Hannibal earned eternal renown.

# George Washington ▶

Maybe it's a stretch to call the father of our country a military genius; he may have lost more battles than he won. As historian Steve Wiegand writes, "His greatest military gifts were in organizing retreats and avoiding devastating losses." But Washington's steadfastness as he battled the planet's most powerful realm with undertrained and underpaid soldiers made him, in historian James Thomas Flexner's famous phrase, "the indispensable man."

In 1775, Washington was named commander of the fledgling Continental Army and dispatched to Boston, which was under British occupation. He soon snuck in 59 cannons from a fort in upstate New York and sent the surprised redcoats retreating to Nova Scotia. But then the empire struck back. Facing an armada and an army numbering 22,000 on Long Island, Washington was driven back, to northern New Jersey. By December 1776, he had lost New York City, two major forts and the confidence of many in the Continental Congress. The British and their Hessian mercenaries closed in for the kill. But when they settled in near Trenton, N.J., Washington, now in Pennsylvania, conceived a bold plan: a river crossing on Christmas night and a surprise attack on Trenton.

Ice floes swirled as the general and some 2,400 men crossed the Delaware River in darkness; not until 4 a.m. were they safely on New Jersey soil. But the gambit worked. The Hessians, after celebrating the holiday with gusto, were easy marks; the flow of the war was reversed. In the months that followed, Washington continued to cleverly avoid head-on battles, instead tying up the enemy in a guerrilla war of attrition that led to final victory in 1781.

# Thomas 'Stonewall' Jackson ▲

Brilliance often walks hand in hand with eccentricity, and Confederate General "Stonewall" Jackson (above, review-ing his troops) is one of military history's most idiosyncratic—and dazzling—examples. The West Point graduate and Mexican-American War veteran was a professor at the Virginia Military Institute in the 1850s, where students mocked him for his religious piety, his boring classroom delivery and his habit of sucking on lemons to relieve his dyspepsia.

But the seeds of military genius require the water of combat to germinate, and Jackson's ripened quickly once the Civil War erupted. He earned his nickname in its first major battle, at Bull Run, where an admiring fellow general declared, "There stands Jackson like a stone wall!" But it was his artful enterprise, his slippery surprise maneuvers and his mastery of logistics that won renown for the once-scorned professor.

Jackson's battlefield creativity was best displayed in his magnificent Valley Campaign in the spring of 1862, when his small force of some 17,000 men led the 60,000 troops of three separate Union armies on a dizzying chase through western Virginia's Shenandoah Valley. The chase successfully kept the Union troops from joining an assault on the Confederate capital, Richmond, Va. Over seven weeks, Jackson's troops marched some 650 miles and fought five major battles, winning four of them.

"Always mystify, mislead and surprise the enemy, if possible," Jackson advised one of his officers. Playing whack-a-mole with the lead-footed Union troops, Jackson's men moved so fast—they were dubbed his "foot cavalry"—that they seemed to vanish in one place only to turn up in another long before it seemed possible. He used a powerful new technology, the railroad, to help fabricate confusion. At one point, he sent his men slogging through mud for three days, leading both the troops and Union spies to believe they were retreating, bound southeast toward Rich-mond and away from the troops of the North's General John C. Frémont, only to suddenly board the men on a long train of boxcars heading westward, right back to the front. General George B. McClellan, commander of the Army of the Potomac, once declared: "I don't like Jackson's movements. He will suddenly appear where least expected." Such was the magic of Professor Stonewall Jackson.

# ◀ Vo Nguyen Giap

His family name, Vo, means "force" in Vietnamese; his given name means "armor." So Vo Nguyen Giap, a onetime history teacher, was only fulfilling his destiny by becoming North Vietnam's top general and router of two mighty armies in a pair of conflicts that spanned 30 years.

Fighting his nation's colonial master, France, after World War II, Giap (center left, behind Ho Chi Minh) mastered guerrilla tactics, using Vietnam's jungles as camouflage, maneuvering his soldiers along hidden trails and tunnels to strike where they were least expected. Moving heavy artillery across lofty mountain passes, his native troops surprised, corralled and besieged a better-equipped occupying force of 12,000 in the stronghold of Dien Bien Phu in 1954. When he finally overran it, Giap became the first modern commander to drive a white European nation out of Asia, and TIME declared that he "shares with China's Mao Zedong a reputation as the world's foremost practitioner of the dark art of insurgency warfare."

Giap was soon using his dark art to face down a tougher foe. By 1966, more than 500,000 U.S. troops were "incountry" supporting their anticommunist allies in South Vietnam. Giap countered with what TIME called "the most cumbersome logistical system since Hannibal brought his elephants over the Alps." To logistical mastery, Giap added methodical preparation, heavy reliance on firepower, willingness to take high casualties, and the ability to weld both guerrillas and regular army forces into a single-minded unit—all of it tempered by an extraordinary caution crystallized in this statement: "Strike to win, strike only when success is certain; if it is not, then don't strike."

A dispirited U.S. had withdrawn by the time Giap's tanks rolled into South Vietnam's capital, Saigon, in the last days of April 1975. His victory, 30 years in the making, demonstrates that genius isn't always the result of a single flash of inspiration; it can also be manifest in the relentless application of brilliant strategy and tactics.

---

# William H. McRaven ▶

Different eras demand different talents, and Admiral William H. McRaven, commander of the U.S. Special Operations Command, has mastered those required to fight a foe unlike any the U.S. has encountered before: the terrorist groups around the world that have waged war against America and its allies in recent decades.

McRaven, who led the secret raid into Pakistan that killed Osama bin Laden in 2011, codified an approach to "special ops," the clandestine actions called for in fighting such a widely dispersed host of enemies, most of whom are deeply embedded in the cultures and villages of their native lands. In fact, he wrote the book on the subject. His *Special Ops: Case Studies in Special Operations Warfare* lays out a six-point checklist for all such missions: surprise, speed, security, simplicity, purpose and repetition. For the bin Laden raid, the *Washington Post* reported, he added one more: precision.

Covert operations weren't a top priority of U.S. troops until the humiliating failure of the raid ordered by President Jimmy Carter in 1980 to free American hostages in Tehran. Today McRaven commands a variety of special-ops units that emerged as a result, and they are the vanguard of the U.S. war on terror, including the U.S. Army's Rangers, Green Berets and Delta Force and the famed U.S. Navy SEALs—McRaven's old outfit and the one he chose to take out bin Laden.

Previously, the square-jawed Texan served in Afghanistan as head of the Joint Special Operations Command, the U.S. covert strike force in the region. Targeting key terrorists with a series of stunning, mostly nighttime raids, he erased entire layers of al Qaeda and Taliban leadership. As Michael G. Vickers, undersecretary of defense for intelligence, declared: "He has taken what was already a very integrated, interagency organization to another level. Bill is a great leader but also a pretty big thinker. It's a rare balance of these two skills."

# PROFOUND PARTNERS

BY DAVID BJERKLIE

*How many people does it take to screw in—or even make—a lightbulb? Works of collaborative genius argue for two heads being better than one*

THERE IS NO SUCH THING AS A GENIUS. OKAY, YOU'RE RIGHT; THAT'S TOO STRONG. HOW ABOUT this: there is no such thing as a lone genius. Sure, some hermit savant could argue that's going too far the other way. The point is, collaboration is the rule in matters of transformative innovation and idea generation. We can all rattle off the most obvious genius-birthing pairings: John Lennon and Paul McCartney; James Watson and Francis Crick; Pierre and Marie Curie; the Marx Brothers. But Albert Einstein and Pablo Picasso got by with a little help from their friends, too. Some people would argue that collaboration is just what human brains do, whether we're aware of it or not.

There are probably some deep-seated reasons we choose to see history in terms of charismatic heroes and villains rather than as a more inclusive tectonic shifting of social forces. Certainly it makes for a better story. The 19th-century Scottish historian Thomas Carlyle put it pretty succinctly: "The history of the world is but the biography of great men." And if this Great Man storyboarding has taken a critical beating of late, we can't quite shake its influence. It's a sexy narrative. We want our geniuses to stand tall—and alone.

Howard Gardner, the author of *Extraordinary Minds* who is known for his theory of multiple intelligences, says it is, however, possible to tread a more sensible middle path. He believes we can recognize the crucial roles of chance, historical forces, and the social needs of a time and place and still accept that "much of the good, and much of the bad, is a result of the thoughts and actions of a few extraordinary individuals." Simply put, great individuals don't exist in a vacuum, and neither do their great achievements. But folks can get almost hostile when someone suggests otherwise. In her book *Creative Collaboration*, Vera John-Steiner calls out the irate audience member at one of her lectures who asked if she "was committed to destroying Western civilization." In the opinion of the inquisitor and many like him, our deepest cultural values hinge on the undisputed importance of individual achievement. Elevating collaboration is a slap in the face to the spirit of self-reliance.

**PLAY MATES**
*The brains behind the Broadway megahit* Book of Mormon *(from left): Trey Parker, Robert Lopez and Matt Stone*

**INTERTWINED** *Science lends itself well to the art of collaboration. James Watson (left) and Francis Crick built on work by Erwin Chargaff and tapped Maurice Wilkins and Rosalind Franklin to discover that DNA exists as a double helix.*

But no matter how in thrall we are to the notion of the lone-wolf genius, reality speaks more for the importance of the pack.

CONSIDER THE LIGHTBULB—THE ICONIC CARTOON version that glows overhead when insight strikes. How appropriate that it was given to us by the Genius of Menlo Park himself, Thomas Edison. Unquestionably a brilliant inventor, Edison had less-heralded talents in visionary management, and his greatest creation might well be the modern industrial research lab. An "invention factory," he called it, and its legacy can be seen in AT&T Bell Labs, Xerox PARC, IBM, NASA's Jet Propulsion Lab, Google and on and on, to wherever today's most defining advances are conceived. Says Keith Sawyer, author of *Group Genius*: "Forget the myths; the truth

is always a story of group genius. If you scratch the surface of any one of these stories, you quickly discover there was a whole lot of collaboration going on." And that's the case, paradoxically, even at an individual level. "Researchers have discovered," says Sawyer, "that even the insights that emerge when you're completely alone can be traced back to previous collaborations."

Once we forget the myths, we can clearly see how individual brilliance is enhanced, not diluted, by collaboration. Erik Demaine is a perfect example. In 2001, at the age of 20, Demaine, who had entered college at 12, completed his Ph.D. and joined the faculty of MIT as a professor of computer science, the youngest professor ever hired by the university. Two years later, he won the MacArthur Fellowship commonly known as the genius grant. Demaine, whose research interests range from theoretical computer science and the geometry of protein folding to the connections between mathematics and art (he has sculptures in the permanent collection of the Museum of Modern Art in New York), is undeniably a rare mind. Yet he is compelled to work with others. He does it on a daily basis with his father, Martin, a technical instructor and artist-in-residence at MIT. But even more to the point, he has cowritten papers with an astounding number of others, 320 and counting.

Demaine has the brains to see the brawn in numbers. "In science everyone has a different background, a different tool set for how to solve problems," he says. "Problems in general tend to break down into pieces, into subproblems. And my theory is, for every subproblem, there's somebody in the world for whom it is trivial. So if you get the right mix of people, you can solve all the subproblems necessary for some big problem." Another attraction of collaboration for Demaine—who, the MacArthur grant noted, had a knack for "moving readily between the theoretical and the playful, with a keen eye to revealing the former in the latter"—is the sheer fun of it.

The joy of collaboration has plenty of precedents, even in mathematics. "Probably the most famous example in my world," says Demaine, "is Paul Erdös, one of the great mathematicians of the 20th century and the one who had the most coauthors [more than 500]. Collaboration was his lifestyle. He was nomadic, traveling around the world to stay with various mathematicians. When he visited someone, he'd say, 'So, do you have any problems?' He just loved to collaborate."

While there are likely few in the academic world who have embraced the power of "we" as wholeheartedly as Erdös, science has seen many other remarkable partnerships, not the least of which were the most intimate. The Curies are certainly the standard-bearers for family-that-works-together success, but did you know that their daughter Irène was also a scientist who, like her parents, shared a Nobel Prize with her spouse? (Irène was married to Jean Frédéric Joliot, who had worked in Marie's radium lab in Paris; their Nobel was also for work with radioactive elements.) Scientists Carl and Gerty Cori also shared Nobels as a married couple. Physicist Lawrence Bragg, who at 25 was the youngest Nobelist ever, won the award with his father, William.

Partnerships, of course, need not be forged by marriage or blood ties, nor are they limited to the sciences. From the 1920s to the 1950s, German playwright and director Bertolt Brecht worked with a long list of the most important figures in European theater, film and music, including composer Kurt Weill. (Both Brecht and Weill also had pivotal artistic partnerships with their respective spouses, actress Helene Weigel and actress and singer Lotte Lenya.) Musical theater,

**MISSION ACCOMPLISHED**
*A battalion of rocket scientists celebrate the daring and complex landing of NASA's Curiosity rover on the surface of Mars in August 2012.*

in fact, has always been especially rich in synergy, probably because there is such a neat division of labor between composer and lyricist. Audiences in the 19th century sang along to the operettas of Gilbert and Sullivan; in the 20th century, Broadway bopped to the musicals of Richard Rodgers in pairings with both Lorenz Hart and Oscar Hammerstein II (who also collaborated with Jerome Kern). Classics were also spun from the pianos and pens of, among others, Betty Comden and Adolph Green, Alan Jay Lerner and Frederick Loewe, and Andrew Lloyd Webber and Tim Rice. Most recently, Trey Parker and Matt Stone (creators also of the game-changing animated TV series *South Park*) sat with director Robert Lopez to develop the musical juggernaut *The Book of Mormon*.

The roll call is even longer in the realm of popular music, where there are almost as many arguments about whether a creative pair adds up to genius as there are creative pairs. Lennon and McCartney, sure. Ditto Duke Ellington and Billy Strayhorn. But how about Gerry Goffin and Carole King? Burt Bacharach and Hal David? Mick Jagger and Keith Richards? Do Elton John and Bernie Taupin make the grade? Or Bono and the Edge? Any takers for ABBA's Benny Andersson and Bjorn Ulvaeus?

Certainly there are few more colossal figures in the recording industry than Quincy Jones, and he would never have achieved his exalted status by himself. In his career as a producer, conductor and arranger, he has won nearly 30 Grammy awards and produced the best-selling album of all time, Michael Jackson's *Thriller*. The nature of his job, though, ensures that none of his creations are his alone. And while jazz trumpeter Miles Davis was a singular talent, his lega-

**DYNAMIC DUO** *Though filled with towering solo figures, some of the best jazz has been made by talented pairs or all-star teams. Duke Ellington (left) called pianist and composer Billy Strayhorn his "writing and arranging companion."*

**IN THEIR BLOOD** *History is sprinkled with families whose combined efforts produced genius. Chico, Harpo and Groucho Marx starred in three films that made the American Film Institute's list of 100 Funniest American Movies of All Time.*

cy as a genius may be stronger for his collaborations. According to writers Andy Boynton and Bill Fischer in their book *Virtuoso Teams,* Davis "revolutionized music at least three times over 30 years, each time working with a different 'all-star' team that he had personally assembled and led."

Collaboration can yield beauty, but that doesn't mean it's always pretty. *West Side Story* transformed American musical theater, but as Boynton and Fischer point out, it took nearly a decade of false starts and clashes of talents and egos among Jerome Robbins, Leonard Bernstein, Arthur Laurents and Stephen Sondheim to make it happen.

Less-fraught dream teams have loomed particularly large in comedy, at least since Groucho, Chico and Harpo made it the family business. The writers' room that powered Sid Caesar's *Your Show of Shows* in the 1950s was a group of Hall of Fame funnymen: Mel Brooks, Woody Allen, Neil Simon, Carl Reiner. Together they created a pioneering TV variety series. Another member of that defining group, Larry Gelbart, who went on to create the TV staple *MASH,* has compared it with a jazz ensemble: "Except for the fact that we were all white and Jewish, we felt like we were the Duke Ellington band," he said. "We had this great sound together." Similarly, since its premiere in 1975,

Lorne Michaels's *Saturday Night Live* has featured the cooperative brilliance (to be honest, sometimes more brilliant than others) of more than 100 per-

COLLABORATION CAN YIELD BEAUTY, BUT THAT DOESN'T MEAN IT'S ALWAYS PRETTY. *WEST SIDE STORY* TOOK NEARLY A DECADE OF EGO CLASHES TO HAPPEN.

formers and writers. While each fan has his favorite ensemble—John Belushi, Gilda Radner, Chevy Chase and Dan Aykroyd; or Jimmy Fallon, Amy Poehler,

**COME TOGETHER** *The Beatles' resident experimentalist John Lennon (left) and the more pop-inclined Paul McCartney were one of the most successful pairs of songwriters in all of music, churning out more than 25 No. 1 hits during the Fab Four's 10-year run.*

Will Ferrell, Tina Fey and Rachel Dratch (or maybe Fred Armisen, Andy Samberg, Bill Hader and Kristen Wiig)—collaboration is the thread that has held the show together throughout. In the world of TV drama, many of us have been riveted by a darker genius—the collaboration of David Simon and Ed Burns on HBO's landmark series *The Wire*.

BRITISH ECONOMIST, BIOGRAPHER and essayist William Skidelsky suggests that our preconceived cultural notions may cloud our judgment about the proper objects of collaboration. Pop songs, musicals, film scripts and TV shows, absolutely. But when it comes to classical music, literary fiction, plays and poems, we are less magnanimous. "The more highbrow the art form, the greater the requirement that it be the work of one person," Skidelsky writes. "We do not like the idea of great art being produced by committee (although we make an exception for the King James Bible)."

But that doesn't mean it doesn't happen. And if the committee meets in secret, or at least beyond our line of sight, we can continue to believe what we want to believe. Picasso is the past century's most innovative and relentless artistic genius; he did it all. Yet his greatest claim to fame, the development of Cubism, was the result of intense collaboration with his French contemporary Georges Braque. According to Vera John-Steiner, many years later Picasso acknowledged to Françoise Gilot, his muse and mother of his children, "Almost every evening I went to Braque's studio or Braque came to mine. Each of us had to see what the other had done during the day. We criticized each other's work. A canvas was not finished until both of us felt it was."

It is also true that we don't always recognize teamwork when

**STREET DREAMS**
*Former* Baltimore Sun *journalist David Simon (left) teamed with former Baltimore police detective Ed Burns to create many works about their beleaguered city. The most famous, of course, was HBO's landmark series* The Wire.

it's right in front of us. Not surprisingly, credit for world-changing accomplishments—or more to the point, the lack thereof—has often followed traditional gender roles. The nature of Einstein's partnership with his first wife, Mileva Maric, has long been the subject of speculation. In their love letters, according to John-Steiner, "they share a dream of common interests and scientific collaboration." To what extent did Maric, who was also a student at the Swiss Polytechnic Institute, participate in her husband's early theorizing? Was she simply a sounding board or something more?

Too often we are willing to view female collaborators as little more than able assistants. Complicating that default assumption is the fact that women often do start out in supportive roles. It seemed to take a while for even Ariel Durant, the wife and work partner of Will Durant, to recognize herself as equal coauthor of their 11-volume classic, *The Story of Civilization*. For much of artist Christo's career, his installations were

credited to him alone. Only after 1994 did his wife, Jeanne-Claude, begin to retroactively get her due.

IF THERE IS A KIT FOR CREATIVITY, THEN, COLLABOration is most definitely a tool in the box. Which makes the question of what the ingredients are for collaborative success a critical one. The key, says Sawyer, is "cognitive diversity." Teams are most likely to exhibit genius when they are "composed of people who have different cognitive material in their minds, different concepts, different backgrounds, different ways of thinking about problems." Add to that intellectual breadth and depth an ability to connect to other people with different areas of breadth and depth. It bears emphasis, says Sawyer, that these characteristics fuel success not only for formally organized groups. In all kinds of ways we collaborate with others—peers and teachers, both present and past. Keeping that in mind could increase the odds that any one of us might play a role in coming up with something brilliant.

# GENIUS AMONG US

# AND . . . THEY'RE OFF!

**BY REGINA NUZZO**

*Your kids are cute and all, but they aren't going to graduate from college before they're 13. Yes, prodigies do get off to fast starts. But where do they finish?*

ALL THINGS CONSIDERED, IT'S A NICE MOMENT TO BE A CHILD PRODIGY. AS A SOCIETY, WE'RE FORKing over tens of thousands of dollars to own the precocious daubs of painters who are adorably missing their baby teeth, flocking to Carnegie Hall to listen to pint-size pianists who need help reaching the pedals, and snapping up books about mathematicians for whom shaving is a distant goal. But for most of human history, prodigies haven't had it this good. Until recently, they were more likely to be considered possessed, not blessed. Bewildered adults fell back on prophecy, sorcery, astrology or reincarnation to explain why the toddler in their midst could speak more languages than they could. In fact, the word prodigy derives from the Latin *prodigium*, which means something unnatural, a monster. "They were viewed with suspicion, awe and fear," says author Andrew Solomon, whose bestseller *Far from the Tree: Parents, Children, and the Search for Identity* includes a chapter on prodigies. "There is something very unsettling about the spectacle of someone who can perform so early and so well."

**CHECKMATE** *Phiona Mutesi—from the slums of Kampala, Uganda—shocked the chess world by becoming her country's under-20 champ and an international phenom.*

We're well beyond assuming demonic involvement when a 4-year-old masters calculus, thank goodness, but scientists still have trouble explaining such unusual achievement. Some new studies are helping to slowly piece together what makes a prodigy so prodigious. Surprising insights about the qualities that kid geniuses share—and the ones they don't—shed light on how they interact with the world, speak to whether these gifts are born or made, and may help the rest of us understand our own more modest gifts.

Most researchers agree that a prodigy is a child who, between the ages of 10 and 13, is already performing at an adult professional level in a highly demanding and valued field. So says David Henry Feldman, child-development professor at Tufts University and coauthor of *Nature's Gambit: Child Prodigies and the Development of Human Potential*. In truth, they are usually obvious at a much earlier age. "If you need to ask whether your child is a prodigy, then she probably isn't," says Ellen Winner, psychology professor at Boston College and author of *Gifted Children: Myths and Reality*. In other words, you'll know a prodigy when you see one, probably by the time he or she is 5 or so—after you've had occasion to retrieve your jaw from the floor, where it's dropped in astonishment.

Take Kim Ung-Yong from South Korea, for example, who could read four languages and solve integral calculus problems by his fourth birthday. Or David Gil, who was 5 when he played the piano at Carnegie Hall. Or William James Sidis, who was accepted into Harvard at 9. "Some of these children are talking at 6 months and reading by the age of 2," says Joanne

Ruthsatz, prodigy researcher and psychology professor at Ohio State University at Mansfield. "That's not normal even in a gifted population."

Such staggering accomplishments make the following fact all the more shocking: you don't need a high IQ to be a prodigy. Middling-to-pretty-good smarts will do just fine. Ruthsatz calculated IQ scores among a sample of documented prodigies and found them to fall between 100 and 147. With 130 typically the threshold for "gifted," that means many of these prodigies were of just normal intelligence. The thing about kids with really high IQs, Ruthsatz says, is that they're typically good at many things and thus may not get around to applying themselves to any one of them until they're older. Prodigies, however, find a way to excel in a specific area at a very young age.

What's their secret? An ironclad working memory, for starters. In Ruthsatz's recent analysis of eight

**HEAD STARTS** *Kim Ung-Yong (top left) conquered calculus by the time he was 4; Michael Kearney (bottom left) was a guest of Jay Leno's after graduating from college at age 10; and pianist Ervin Nyiregyhazi (above) was 8 when he performed at Buckingham Palace.*

but also on writing it down, Mozart was summoned by the Pope. Legend has it that instead of threatening the virtuoso with excommunication, the Pope was so impressed that he simply praised young Wolfie and sent him on his way.

But while that was surely an impressive feat of memory (if true), would we still be repeating the story if the boy had not grown up to give us the beautiful *Eine kleine Nachtmusik*? "Prodigies are not necessarily creative," Feldman says. "Mozart was in this sense an exception, a rarity even among the very rare." That's why prodigies tend to crop up most often in rule-based domains like music, math and chess, where little squirts with big memories can conquer the necessary patterns and quickly rise to the top through technical mastery. Poetry, literature and the visual arts, on the other hand, require more creativity, emotional depth and life experience—ingredients far less likely to be in the cupboard of a youngster who hasn't yet hit puberty.

Mozart and his stage father aside, prodigies are more bulldog than pampered poodle, driven as they are by fierce internal fires. They've got a "rage to learn," says Kevin Kearney, who should know. He is the father of Michael, who graduated from high school at 6 and from college at 10. In fact, in the prodigy's household, the parents find themselves trying to shoo their tykes out the door, begging them for heaven's sake to get outside and play, while the children ask if they can please just download all the MIT physics lectures first. "Prodigies tap into something that's fundamentally human," says Scott Barry Kaufman, author of *Ungifted: Intelligence Redefined*. "What they're doing is an extension of themselves. They've found their love at a very early age. It's play for them." Kaufman calls it entering a flow state, an experience of joyful absorption during which mundane concerns like meals, school and bedtime recede into the background.

This is a world in which beauty lies in the details. One mathematics prodigy in Ruthsatz's study insisted on correcting an astronomy lecturer at the local university about the exact distance from Mars to Earth; he was 3 years old. Another reported that sometimes he pretends not to remember too many fine points because it worries the grown-ups. "People assume I must be thinking about them 24/7," he says. "It's just that I can remember every detail of the past." Ruthsatz's prodigies scored even higher on attention to detail than another group that is defined by it: children with Asperger's, an autism-spectrum disorder.

None of this magic happens in a vacuum, of course.

prodigies, all scored at least in the 99th percentile in tests of working memory, with six maxing out at 99.9. This kind of memory not only stores information but analyzes it, which is trickier than it sounds. Imagine if someone were to read you a fairy tale, for instance, and then ask you to repeat back every fifth word. Now substitute "secret choral chants" for "fairy tale" and you have an actual storied example of prodigious working memory in action. According to most versions of the tale, during a trip to Rome, 14-year-old Wolfgang Amadeus Mozart listened to a performance of Gregorio Allegri's famous and jealously guarded *"Miserere"* choir piece at the Sistine Chapel. When he returned to his room later that night, he transcribed the entire score from memory. Because there was a papal ban not only on performing the piece elsewhere

"97-Year-Old Dies Unaware of Being Violin Prodigy," trumpets a headline in the newspaper parody *The Onion*. Funny, but sadly true: innate gifts aside, you're never going to be a violin prodigy unless you're lucky enough to find a violin. Look at Phiona Mutesi, who at age 9 was on the brink of starvation in the slums of Uganda when she stumbled into a building that promised a free bowl of porridge to kids who sat down and learned a mysterious game with black and white pieces on a square board. Chess immediately became her obsession. Within a year, Mutesi had beaten her coach. Within two, she'd won the Uganda women's junior championship. By 19 she was titled by the World Chess Federation.

Clearly, prodigies move fast, faster than the rest of us. But their head start doesn't always take them farther. The Japanese have a proverb: "The 10-year-old prodigy becomes a talented 15-year-old on the way to mediocrity at 20." Solomon concurs: "I think that prodigies are noteworthy for how fast they develop rather than how profoundly they develop," he says. "It's always a mistake to confound speed and depth. There are some people who show remarkable early ability and then go on to change the world, but many who develop early don't have access to genius." What's important, he says, is whether they get proper nurturing from parents and teachers and are protected from exploitation and overexposure. The early-20th-century piano prodigy Ervin Nyiregyhazi, for example, was allowed to remain so focused on his training that he reportedly could not tie his own shoelaces when he was 21.

There are those, in fact, who argue that we do our prodigies no favors. "Maybe we shouldn't be making such a big deal about precocity," Kaufman says. "There's something to be said for wisdom. I cringe every time another article comes out with a headline like '5-Year-Old Genius Can Read Shakespeare.' Simply being ahead of his peers doesn't make him a genius. Early mastery is just a small part of eventual greatness."

In the end, prodigies are, in some very real ways, just like the rest of us. According to Kaufman, we all need to learn the same unglamorous if no less important lessons, the ones that can't be memorized but rather reveal themselves only by doing: how to fail without falling to pieces, build meaningful human relationships, benefit from supportive and challenging mentors, handle—and continually grow from—criticism. These gifts, he says, may never make one a prodigy. But they will help to make one human.

# THE GIFTED GROW UP

*A violinist, a medical whiz and a mathematician describe what it's like to begin life as a child prodigy—and what happens next*

**Tony Hansberry, 19, Tallahassee, Fla.**
In seventh grade, I competed in my school's science fair. I didn't place. So the next year I really focused on trying to make a winning project. I'd interned at the University of Florida's Shands Hospital over the previous two summers, so I went back to get some inspiration. I spoke with an ob-gyn who suggested I do a project about hysterectomy removals. In less than a week, I'd figured out a new stitching technique that allowed for a faster procedure time and fewer complications. I was pretty surprised by the reactions to it. The story was first reported in the local paper, and it wasn't long before I was on local TV. It opened up a lot of doors for me. Now I attend Florida A&M, because that's where my father went. Although I am focused on my goal of being a trauma surgeon, I'm not just stuck in a room reading a book. I'm a regular teenager. I go to parties. The only difference is, I can be grateful for already having been held up as a success story.

**BOY WONDER** *Tony Hansberry (right, in ninth grade) perfects his hysterectomy sewing technique.*

### Brianna Kahane, 11, Delray Beach, Fla.

I was 2½ when my mom realized I had an ear for music. We were in a department store and I recognized the classical piece playing in the background; it was from one of my Baby Einstein videos. Mom was pretty freaked out. But soon she was encouraging my talent and taking me to concerts. I loved the sound of the violin from the beginning. It wasn't long before I was begging for one of my own. My mom finally gave in, getting one off eBay for me when I was 4.

People began to notice I had some really special musical gifts, like perfect pitch and a photographic memory. Eventually, I got the chance to play for both President Clinton and Oprah; that was the time of my life—she was so sweet to me! About two years ago, I decided to try out for Juilliard. I was so psyched to audition; I knew a lot of really good people had gone there. When I got accepted, I felt so fortunate. Over the years, I've played for *a lot* of people, but I still feel like a regular girl with a really big dream: to become a world-class violinist. My schedule is just like everybody else's, except I have more practicing to do. I still have time to play with my kitten and friends, though.

**FRESH SOUND** *Now 11, Brianna Kahane is a student at Juilliard.*

### Harvey Friedman, 84, Columbus, Ohio

My parents were in the phototypesetting business, but I wasn't encouraged to follow them. Instead they had me concentrate on mathematics and music. I remember looking at our grocery bill and adding up the numbers in different orders—like, $1 + 2 + 3 = 3 + 2 + 1$—and always getting the same sum. And I wanted to understand why that was true. When I was 11, I went to summer school at the University of Oklahoma and received a perfect score on a final exam in calculus. So the school arranged for me to have additional study time to work on math and also suggested that I skip a grade. Later I took summer courses at Northwestern University in various math topics before being admitted to the Massachusetts Institute of Technology in 1964. I hadn't yet turned 16—and I hadn't even received my high school diploma.

When I arrived on campus, I immediately contacted a well-known philosophy professor there to ask him some questions that had been bothering me. Since logic is the basis of all deductive reasoning, how does logic itself start? Or is deductive reasoning inherently

**FAST TRACK** *Shortly after earning his Ph.D. at MIT, Harvey Friedman became Stanford's youngest professor, at 18.*

circular? Those questions still remain unresolved for me. I thrived in my classes, though. During my time at MIT, I began to formulate Ph.D.-level projects, and all that self-generated research sped me along a path that allowed me to become a math graduate student without having to first get a bachelor's degree.

At 18, I was offered a position at Stanford University as an assistant professor of philosophy, teaching graduate students whose average age was about 24. Despite the age discrepancy, the course went smoothly. But I also taught an undergraduate course in logic, and that was a different matter. I gave a true-or-false exam, and the median score came in around 15 out of 100. There was a lot of unhappiness. Turns out, most students looked at the educational experience differently than I did. I was fine with right and wrong; they preferred partial credit. I then got appointments at universities in Wisconsin and New York before settling in at Ohio State University in 1977 as a professor of mathematics until my retirement last year. These days, I'm working on a math project I've been trying to solve for decades and spending more time with my music. I've had a nice run. Still, looking back, I do think I could have benefited from having more academically oriented parents. I would have arrived at MIT thinking a lot more clearly about mathematics and science and been much better suited to taking advantage of my opportunities.

*Reported by Lena Finkel & Jenisha Watts*

"A genius is somebody whose work shows the existence of a rich inner life, but because of this you can't always tell when you meet one whether she is a genius or not. I don't think it's possible for a writer to just pop off great works. Great works require an enormous amount of discipline and commitment. Only certain personalities—a very determined person, or someone who stumbles upon a reason to become determined—can realize their gifts. A work of genius has to be deep, and it is deep when all of its parts relate to one another to create a singular vision. This vision can only come from a writer with the deepest inner resources. Sometimes the writer herself isn't aware of these resources, and certainly there are times when those of us working with a writer can't tell if those resources are there. A lot of writers in our program are absentminded. Many simply don't pay attention to deadlines and phone messages, bills or mail. They're not living in what I call logistical time; they're living in an inner time, not really here in the way that the world expects them to be. In fact, some of the most gifted people I've encountered are some of the least functional. Of course, some extremely gifted people are quite functional. But I do think that to write something powerful, it's necessary to disconnect from logistical time."

**—SAMANTHA CHANG,**
**Director, University of Iowa**
**Writers' Workshop**

# HOW TO SPOT

"First of all, genius is not visible, so you can't 'spot' one. To qualify for membership in Mensa, you have to score in the top 2% on a standardized intelligence test. That's a worldwide standard. Certainly, though, it is not the only marker. I have absolutely no doubt that my plumber is a real genius when it comes to knowing about how my sink works, and an IQ test won't necessarily confirm that at all. Spotting genius, in the end, has to do with what type of expertise you are actually looking for."

**—PAM DONAHOO,**
**Executive Director,**
**American Mensa**

*Isn't there a test for that? Sometimes, sure. But those who are in the business of discovering supreme talent say they depend more on inkling*

**REPORTED BY**
**JENISHA WATTS**

# A GENIUS

"YOU'VE HEARD STRING INSTRUMENTS IN STUDENT ORCHESTRAS—THEY'RE NOT QUITE IN TUNE AND VERY ANNOYING. SO CERTAINLY THE FIRST ISSUE IS: ARE THEY PLAYING IN TUNE NATURALLY OR DOES IT LOOK LIKE A STRUGGLE? THE NEXT CONCERN IS INTUITIVE MUSICAL SHAPING. DOES THEIR PHRASING SOUND NATURAL? DOES IT IMPLY DRAMA AND CALMNESS? DOES IT INCLUDE VARIETY AND VIBRATO? THE THIRD CONSIDERATION IS EASY PHYSICAL COORDINATION. YOU CAN LOOK AT A PERSON AND SEE QUICKLY IF HE IS WORKING TOO HARD TO CONTROL HIS INSTRUMENT. HOW DOES HE HOLD THE VIOLIN? HOW DOES HE MOVE THE BOW? SOME VIOLINISTS ARE DESCRIBED AS LOOKING AS IF THE INSTRUMENT IS PART OF THEIR BODY. IT TAKES EXTRAORDINARY TALENT TO CREATE THAT ILLUSION, PARTLY BECAUSE THE HARDER YOU WORK, THE LESS CONVINCING YOU LOOK. YOU SEE IT IN TENNIS PLAYERS. YOU SEE IT VIRTUALLY EVERYWHERE, REALLY. SOME PEOPLE LOOK NATURAL, SOME LOOK CLUMSY. COMMUNICATION WITH THE AUDIENCE IS CRUCIAL TOO. LOTS OF KIDS LEARN ALL THE NOTES AND HAVE THE RHYTHM EXACTLY RIGHT, YET THEIR MUSIC SOUNDS WOODEN. IT DOESN'T FLOW. AND FINALLY, MAYBE THE MOST ARBITRARY CRITERION OF ALL IS RHYTHMIC STABILITY. MUSIC CAN'T RUSH, IT CAN'T DRAG, IT HAS TO FEEL, YES, NATURAL. DOES THIS TELL YOU HOW TO SPOT A GENIUS? I DON'T KNOW, BUT IT WILL IDENTIFY AN EXTRAORDINARILY GIFTED MUSICIAN."

—STEPHEN CLAPP, Dean Emeritus, The Juilliard School

# ORDINARY BRILLIANCE

BY ELLEN SHAPIRO

*If da Vinci was so smart, why didn't he invent Velcro? Because you could do it*

THE MODEL-T, PENICILLIN, iDEVICES—YOUR BASIC EARTH-shattering inventions usually arrive courtesy of history's rarest thinkers. But what about some of our less attention-grabbing, more get-through-the-day products? Whose ideas were Band-Aids, or Bubble Wrap? A surprising amount of innovation has sprung from the regular minds of regular Joes and Joannas—homemakers, secretaries and moonlighting engineers. Their ingenious, if sometimes accidental, breakthroughs shape our world, too.

### Adhesive bandage ▶

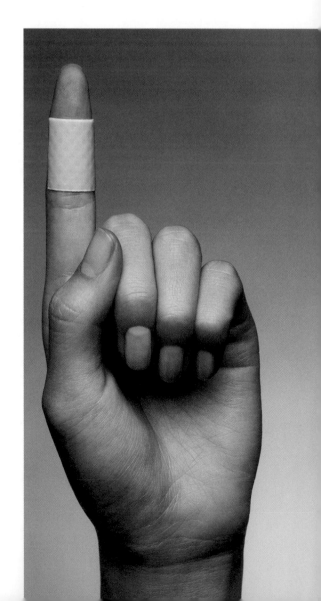

Josephine Dickson had butterfingers in the kitchen and lots of nicks to show for it, but wound care in 1920 meant wrestling to cut a suitable length of gauze and another of tape from a larger spool before applying. That's asking a lot of someone who's bleeding and alone. Josephine's new husband, **Earle Dickson**, a cotton buyer for Johnson & Johnson, got used to coming home to patch her up before dinner, but that was no way to begin a marriage. He envisioned long strips of surgical tape with gauze already affixed to its center and a layer of crinoline between them to keep them from sticking together. Earle's bosses at J&J saw the possibilities, but their Band-Aids didn't catch on until the company began to give them away to the Boy Scouts. Dickson made vice president—and klutzes around the globe began to heal a lot faster.

## ◀ Rolling suitcase

There's a reason you can't spell luggage without l-u-g. Before 1970 you'd grab the handle, dead-lift your bag, and stagger to the curb or down the hall. An empathetic suitcase-company executive, **Bernard Sadow**, tried to ease travelers' pain by adding casters and a long strap. Problem was, his configuration left the suitcase horizontal, which meant pulling it like a disobedient leashed dog. Years later, in 1987, Northwest Airlines pilot **Bob Plath** placed his bag in the upright position, then added larger wheels and a telescoping handle. Not long after, fellow crew members gave it a thumbs-up, Plath founded Travelpro International, and the flying public was soon gliding to their planes, trains and buses ahead of their Rollaboards.

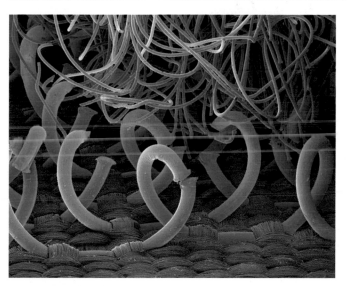

## ◀ Velcro

If it weren't for **George de Mestral**'s dog, we'd never know that satisfying *vrrrrrrrp* sound when Velcro is peeled apart. In 1941 the Swiss engineer was engaged in removing burrs that stuck to his pet's coat after a walk in the woods. Inspecting their tiny hooks, he was inspired to create a synthetic version by combining a fabric strip with thousands of similar hooks with another that had thousands of loops. Velcro—the trade name is an amalgam of the French words *velours* (velvet) and *crochet* (hook)—finally blasted off in the 1960s after NASA astronauts used it to keep things from floating around the space capsule. It's been assisting gravity here on Earth ever since.

## Slinky ▶

"A spring, a spring, a marvelous thing," said the renowned jingle, but who knew until one was unceremoniously knocked off a shelf. In 1943, a mechanical engineer named **Richard James** was experimenting with springs as a cushion for sensitive equipment on ships. When he accidentally toppled one, it didn't fall straightaway but instead "walked" over a stack of books and a tabletop before recoiling upon reaching the floor. James saw little-kid potential, and his wife, Betty, plucked just the right name for his discovery out of the dictionary. When they debuted their Slinky at Gimbel's department store in Philadelphia, they sold out their stock of 400 in 90 minutes. Production revved up once Richard invented the machine that manufactures each Slinky out of 80 feet of steel wire wound into 2½-inch spirals. So far, that translates into enough wire to circle the earth 150 times.

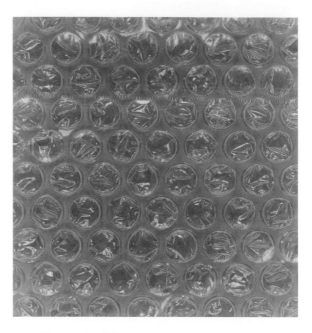

## Sports bra ▲

What on earth would a frustrated female runner do with a couple of jockstraps? Make the world's first JogBra, of course. In 1977 the jogging craze was in full stride, but women were slowed by their droopy-strapped—and thus painfully not shock-absorbing—support garments. One avid athlete, **Lisa Lindahl**, set out to solve the problem with costume designer **Polly Smith**, but their aha! moment didn't come until Lindahl's husband jokingly modeled a jockstrap around his chest. Smith sewed two together, and a bra was born. The supportive undergarment quickly graduated beyond runners' world. Cited as a driver of the women's sports boom, the first JogBra resides in the permanent costume collections of the Smithsonian and the Metropolitan Museum of Art.

## ▲ Bubble Wrap

It has been made into wedding gowns and volleyballs, and an iPhone app lets you pop it virtually in times of stress. Its first order of business, of course, is as a packing cushion. But that isn't what its inventors originally had in mind. In 1957, all engineers **Marc Chavannes** and **Al Fielding** were trying to do was make plastic wallpaper in a New Jersey garage. As the story goes, Chavannes landed on Bubble Wrap's true calling in an airplane, when he noticed that clouds appeared to cushion the wings during descent. Today, Chavannes and Fielding's company, Sealed Air Corp., sells enough each year to reach to the moon and back. But they know full well that their product has many uses. As the company website, bubblewrapfun.com, advises: "Pop Bubble Wrap to calm down."

## ◀ Liquid Paper

In 1951, **Bette Nesmith Graham** was a single mom supporting her young son (future Monkees guitarist Mike Nesmith) as an executive secretary, and she and her work colleagues were not at all happy with those new electric typewriters that made erasing typos a smudgy mess. One day Graham, a thwarted artist, filled a small bottle with tempera, dipped in a watercolor brush and, with a few strokes, whitewashed away her errors. Her boss didn't notice, which was a good sign for the product's potential. But it was bad for Graham's career—when her boss found out about her side business, she was let go. She perfected "Mistake Out" (later renamed Liquid Paper) at home for years until she could finally open a factory, and by 1968 she was selling a million bottles annually. Gillette bought her company for $47.5 million in 1979, months before she died at age 56.

## ◀ Disposable diapers

**Marion Donovan**, a Connecticut housewife and mother of two, was sick of those leaky cloth diapers, so she pulled out her sewing machine, cut up a shower curtain, attached some snaps, and birthed a waterproof and reusable diaper cover. She called it the Boater and in 1951 sold the rights for $1 million (more than $9 million in today's dollars). But the indefatigable inventor didn't stop there, later designing an absorbent paper that made the diaper itself disposable. For 10 years, manufacturers turned their back(side)s to her idea—and then Pampers finally got it. Busy mothers rejoiced, environmentalists less so; they continue to warn that billions of those "disposable" diapers are clogging our landfills.

## 401(k) ▶

Reading the IRS tax code can make anyone's head spin, but in 1980, benefits consultant **Ted Benna** stuck with it long enough to find an obscure subparagraph. His sharp eye revolutionized American retirement. Section 401(k) legitimizes tax-deferred employee savings plans. The law was drawn up mostly to set up a shelter for high-income executives, but Benna realized it could be creatively interpreted to help the rest of us, too. What resulted was a retirement account that invests a percentage of an employee's pretax wages and—better yet—sweetens the deal with matching company contributions. Here's the thing, though: as ubiquitous as his idea has become (there are now more than 60 million participants), Benna never meant it to be a stand-alone retirement savings plan, only a supplement. Today he is one of many critics who thinks 401(k)s have gotten too complicated and risky.

## ◀ Chocolate-chip cookies

In the early 1930s, **Ruth Graves Wakefield**, who ran the Toll House Inn in Whitman, Mass., was whipping up a batch of Butter Drop Do cookies when she realized that she was out of the baking chocolate she used. She chopped up a bar of Nestlé's Semi-Sweet instead, figuring it, too, would melt fully into the batter. It didn't, and thank goodness. Soon her new treats were wildly popular, and her recipe was being published throughout New England. Ever the businesswoman, Wakefield realized that she had helped to spike Nestlé's sales and struck a deal: the company could print her recipe on its packaging as long as she got all the chocolate she needed for the rest of her life.

# THE LONG, HARD ROAD

BY GEOFF COLVIN

*Not everybody can be a genius, but nobody can be one if he isn't willing to put in the hours and a very particular kind of effort*

JOHANN SEBASTIAN BACH, AMONG THE GREATEST MUSICAL GENIUSES OF ALL TIME, DIDN'T CONSIDER himself one. He explained away his staggering achievements so easily that you have to hesitate to believe him: "I was made to work. If you are equally industrious, you will be equally successful."

Michelangelo, whose artistry is so sublime that words can scarcely do it justice, was "a genius" in the opinion of Giorgio Vasari, a painter and writer who called his friend "a gift from God." But Michelangelo's own position was a lot less high-flown. "If people only knew how hard I work to gain my mastery, it wouldn't seem so wonderful at all," he said.

Tiger Woods is universally regarded as an awesomely talented golfer, maybe the greatest ever. But when he came roaring back with four victories in his first seven starts in 2013—after only three PGA Tour wins in the previous three years—he didn't attribute it to talent. "I needed to get healthy enough where I could practice," he said, referring to his persistent left-knee problems. "I've always been pretty good…when I could practice, and my record reflects that….Now I've been able to do that for the last couple of years, and you can see the results."

Funny thing about genius—as we marvel at the astonishing achievements of the world's greatest performers, we find ourselves stumped by the mysterious origins of their magical abilities. Meanwhile, the geniuses themselves are giving us the answer, if only we'd listen. And they're saying there is nothing mysterious or magical about any of it.

Researchers, who have been studying the phenomenon of genius-level performance with scientific rigor for the past 30 years or so, agree. Of course, they would prefer to not even use the word "genius"; it's too fuzzy. Rather, they focus on "reproducible expert performance," that is, world-class achievement that isn't the product of randomness. Their studies make it quite clear where that expert performance comes from. And where it doesn't.

Despite what the geniuses say, their outsize accomplishments can't be born out of

**STUDIES SHOW**
*that genius-level achievement comes not from innate talent, but from years of hard work and deliberate practice.*

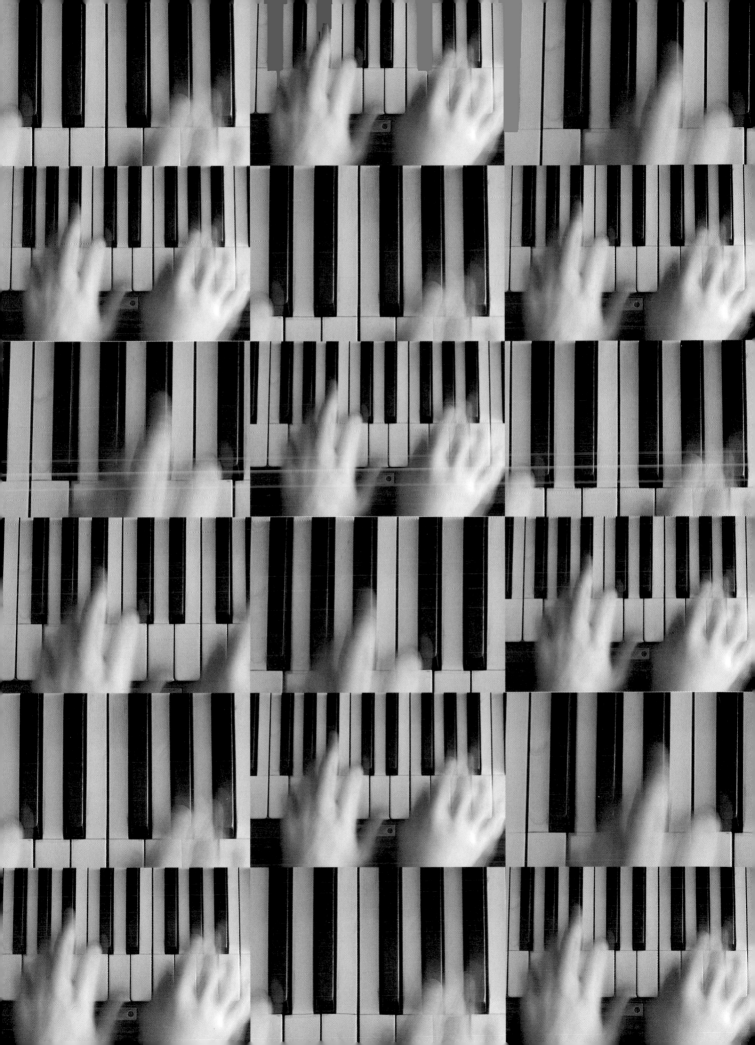

plain hard work. Yes, they work prodigiously, but then so do lots of others, none of whom are world-class performers. There has to be more to it, something specific to the way geniuses work.

Nor is elevated intelligence alone an explanation. We think of chess as an exercise in pure brainpower, for example, but research has found that some grand masters actually have IQs below 100—that is, below average. It's the same story with Go, a Japanese strategy game that is at least as complex as chess. Some top Scrabble players, too, score below average on verbal-ability tests. A brainy IQ isn't the secret to great performance. It isn't even necessary for it.

Most surprisingly, neither is innate ability. The belief that some kind of divine gift is the source of transcendent work doesn't stand up well to scientific scrutiny. Have you ever heard of Patricia Travers or Ferrucio Burco? Probably not—because though they were once musical child prodigies, like so many like them, they didn't grow up to be great adult performers. Similarly, researchers have found that most great adult performers could not have been identified as future geniuses when they were children; they didn't break out until much later. There are, of course, famous exceptions (Tiger Woods, Itzhak Perlman), but for the most part, early signs of genius aren't obvious. And when they are, they're often deceptive.

So brilliance doesn't spring from any of the obvious sources. Where, then, does it come from? It is rooted in what researchers led by K. Anders Ericsson of Florida State University call deliberate practice. And although it does involve lots of hard work—thousands and thousands of hours over many years—deliberate practice is something very different from what the rest of us might think of as practice. Deliberate practice has four main components:

### IT MAKES YOU BETTER AT THE SKILLS YOU NEED AT A PARTICULAR STAGE OF DEVELOPMENT.

Blinding speed is generally considered mandatory in an NFL receiver, for instance, yet Jerry Rice, the greatest pass catcher in football history, wasn't all that speedy. His legendarily grueling workouts focused instead on strengthening the parts of his body that helped him to run precise patterns and change direction suddenly.

### IT PUSHES JUST BEYOND CURRENT ABILITIES.

There is no point in practicing what you have no chance to achieve, because all you will be is overwhelmed and lost. And there is no point in practicing

## OVER AND OVER AGAIN

Even great achievers have to work very hard to get where they are going

◀ Benjamin Franklin
As a boy, "America's first great man of letters" created a meticulous curriculum for himself from magazine articles.

Judit Polgár ▲
The last of three sisters was homeschooled and put through a relentless chess-training regimen by a father who believed top-tier performers are made, not born. The facts don't contradict him. At 15, his daughter became the youngest grandmaster ever.

only what falls within your current ability, because then you won't grow. Instead, deliberate practice puts you in a position to be constantly striving to achieve what is just out of reach. Top-level figure skaters spend most of their practice sessions on jumps they can't quite do, and they fall down a lot—until they don't. And once they don't, they have an expanded repertoire to show for it. Mediocre skaters spend most of their practice on jumps they can more or less do. They don't fall as much, but they don't win medals either.

### IT IS REPEATED AT HIGH VOLUME.

Performing an activity hundreds or thousands of times actually changes the wiring of your brain by building up a substance called myelin. Nerve fibers and neurons work better when they have more myelin covering them. To build up myelin over a nerve fiber that controls, say, striking a particular piano key

Jerry Rice ▲

The best wide receiver in NFL history improved the weaker parts of his game by designing a notoriously rigorous and exhausting practice that focused on skills specific to his position.

◀ Chris Rock

Before his sold-out New Year's Eve show at Madison Square Garden in 2007, Rock tirelessly honed his new material in small comedy clubs around the country.

in a particular way, you need to send the appropriate signal through that fiber many, many times.

**IT PROVIDES CONTINUOUS FEEDBACK.**

There is no getting better without somehow knowing how you are doing, and often we're not good judges of our own performance. That bar of the Brahms Violin Concerto you just played might have sounded perfect to your ears, but what do other ears think about it? Even the world's most accomplished performers have teachers or coaches to critique their work.

Clearly, deliberate practice is extraordinarily demanding, requiring intense focus and concentration. But the very same qualities that make it "deliberate" can make it mentally debilitating. In fact, the work is so arduous that no one can sustain it for long. A finding that is remarkably consistent across disciplines is that four or five hours a day seems to be the upper limit of deliberate practice, and even that much is fre-

quently accomplished only in multiple sessions lasting no more than an hour or 90 minutes each. In fact, elite athletes say the factor that most controls their practice time is the ability to sustain concentration.

At an hour a shot, genius-making is one long slog. Recently, the number that has been riding the pop-culture wind is 10,000: the hours it takes to become special in any given discipline. That figure first turned up in a landmark study of violinists by Ericsson and his colleagues, and it has since been reinforced in many others. But often, discussions of that finding overlook a most important detail: that 10,000 hours isn't of work in general, but rather of deliberate practice. And given how difficult it is to log deliberate practice time, in the end, we're talking about it taking at least 10 years to unleash genius, 10 years of reaching for what can't quite be attained, of making mistakes, of suffering failure. Ericsson minced no words when he said it's "not inherently enjoyable."

Make no mistake, the price paid by a lifetime devoted to deliberate practice is high. Even if one's marriage or other relationships survive, any other outside interests typically do not. Harvard researcher Howard Gardner, in an extensive study of seven creative geniuses including Einstein, Freud, Gandhi, Picasso, and Stravinsky, noted that "usually, as a means of being able to continue work, the creator sacrificed normal relationships in the personal sphere." Such people are "committed obsessively to their work. Social life or hobbies are almost immaterial. . . ." And if that sounds like admirable self-sacrifice and purposeful direction, in fact it can take on ugly overtones. As Gardner observed, "Self-confidence merges with egotism, egocentrism, and narcissism: each of the creators seems highly self-absorbed, not only wholly involved in his or her own projects, but likely to pursue them at the cost of other individuals." The story of the great achiever who leaves a wake of anger and betrayal and often ends up abandoned and alone is no fiction.

But it is exactly that kind of devotion that the special ones have been trying to describe to us all along. Whether they call it deliberate practice or not, that's what it is, and they want us—need us—to see what they put themselves through. Somehow they find a way to drive themselves, compulsively, the next day and every day, pushing, always pushing, for years. That, they are telling us, is where genius comes from.

No wonder it's so rare.

*Adapted from* Talent Is Overrated, *by Geoff Colvin. Penguin Group, 2008*

# THE NEXT AGE OF REASON

BY LEV GROSSMAN

*It's called the Singularity, the moment artificial intelligence surpasses human intelligence and ends civilization as we know it—and it's almost here*

ON FEB. 15, 1965, A DIFFIDENT BUT SELF-POSSESSED HIGH SCHOOL STUDENT NAMED RAYMOND Kurzweil appeared as a guest on a game show called *I've Got a Secret*. He was introduced by the host, Steve Allen, and then played a short musical composition on a piano. Kurzweil was hiding an unusual fact, and the panelists—they included a comedian and a former Miss America—had to guess what it was.

On the show (you can find the clip on YouTube), the beauty queen did a good job of grilling Kurzweil, but the comedian got the win: the music was composed by a computer. Kurzweil got $200.

He then demonstrated the computer, which he had built himself—a desk-size affair, with loudly clacking relays, hooked up to a typewriter. The panelists were pretty blasé about it; they were more impressed by Kurzweil's age than by what he'd actually done. Soon they were content to move on to Mrs. Chester Loney of Rough and Ready, Calif., whose secret was that she'd been President Lyndon Johnson's first-grade teacher.

But Kurzweil would spend much of the rest of his career working out what his demonstration meant. Creating a work of art is one of those activities we reserve for humans and humans only. It's an act of self-expression; you're not supposed to be able to do it if you don't have a self. To see creativity, the exclusive domain of humans, usurped by a computer built by a 17-year-old is to watch a line blur that cannot be unblurred, the line between organic intelligence and artificial intelligence.

That was Kurzweil's real secret, and back in 1965 nobody guessed it. Maybe not even Kurzweil at the time. Now, 48 years later, he believes that we're approaching a moment when computers will become not just intelligent, but more intelligent than humans. When that happens, humanity—our bodies, our minds, our civilizations—will be completely and irreversibly transformed. This moment, he thinks, is not only inevitable but imminent. According to his calculations, the end of human civilization as we know it is about 35 years away.

**FUTURAMA** *There are those who believe that someday soon, humans and machines will become one.*

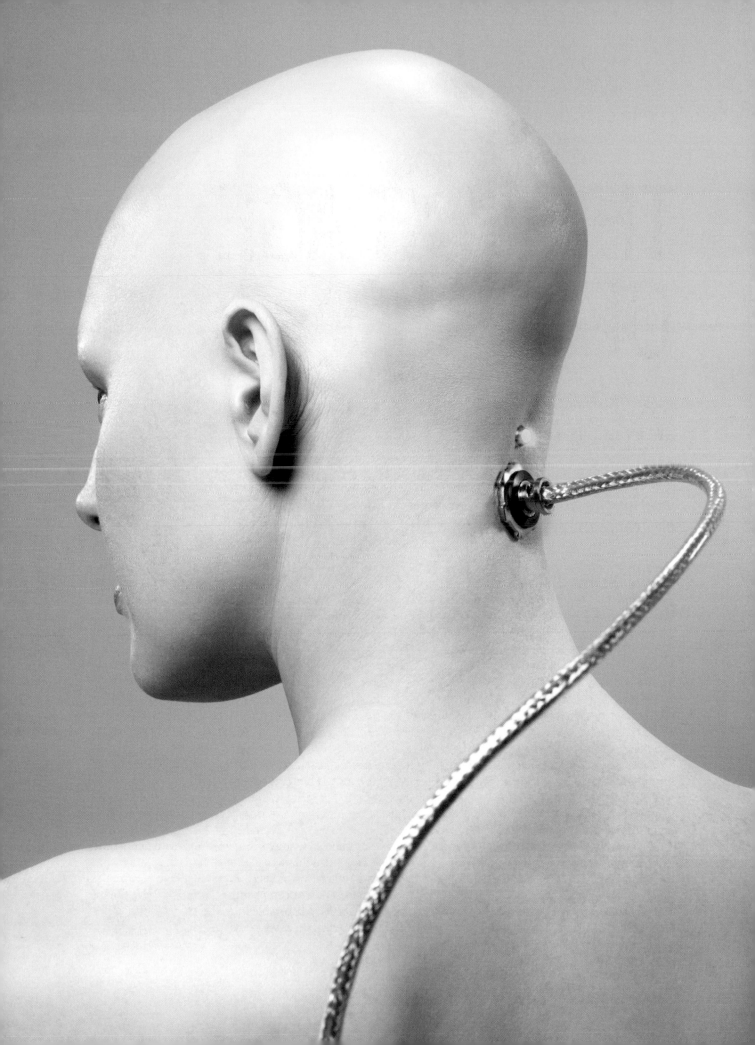

**BIG PICTURE** *Technologist Raymond Kurzweil has a radical vision for humanity's immortal future.*

COMPUTERS ARE GETTING FASTER. EVERYBODY knows that. Also, computers are getting faster *faster*—that is, the rate at which they're getting faster is increasing.

True? True.

So if computers are getting so much faster so incredibly fast, there might conceivably come a moment when they are capable of something compa-rable to human intelligence. Artificial intelligence. All that horsepower could be put in the service of emulating whatever it is our brains are doing when they create consciousness—not just doing arithmetic very quickly or composing piano music, but driving cars, writing books, making ethical decisions, appreciating fancy paintings, making witty observations at cocktail parties.

If you can swallow that idea—and Kurzweil and a lot of other very smart people can—then all bets are off. From that point on, there's no reason to think computers would stop getting more powerful. They would keep on developing until they were far more intelligent than we are. Their rate of development would also continue to increase, because they would take over their own development from their slower-thinking human creators. Imagine a computer scientist that is itself a superintelligent computer. It would work incredibly quickly. It could draw on huge amounts of data effortlessly. It wouldn't even take breaks to play Farmville.

Probably. It's impossible to predict the behavior of these smarter-than-human intelligences with which (with whom?) we might one day share the planet, because if we could, we'd be as smart as they will be. But there are a lot of theories about it. Maybe we'll merge with them to become superintelligent cyborgs, using computers to extend our intellectual abilities in the same way cars and planes extend our physical abilities. Maybe the artificial intelligences will help us treat the effects of old age and prolong our life spans indefinitely. Maybe we'll scan our consciousness into computers and live inside them virtually, as software, forever. Maybe the computers will turn against humanity and annihilate us. The one thing all these theories have in common is the transformation of our species into something that is no longer recognizable as such to us circa 2013. This transformation has a name: the Singularity.

The difficult thing to keep sight of when you're talking about the Singularity is that even though it sounds like science fiction, it isn't, no more than a weather forecast is science fiction. It's not a fringe idea; it's a serious hypothesis about the future of life on Earth. There's an intellectual gag reflex that kicks in when you try to swallow an idea that involves superintelligent, immortal cyborgs, but suppress it if you can, because while the Singularity appears to be on the face of it preposterous, it's a concept that rewards sober, careful evaluation.

People are spending a lot of money trying to understand it. The three-year-old Singularity University, which offers interdisciplinary courses of study for graduate students and executives, is hosted by NASA. Google was a founding sponsor whose CEO and co-founder Larry Page spoke there last year. People are attracted to the Singularity for its shock value, like an intellectual freak show, but they stay because there's more to it than they expected. And of course, in the event that it turns out to be real, it will be the most important thing to happen to human beings since the invention of language.

THE SINGULARITY ISN'T A WHOLLY NEW IDEA, JUST newish. In 1965 the British mathematician I.J. Good described what he called an intelligence explosion: "Let an ultraintelligent machine be defined as a machine that can far surpass all the intellectual activities of any man, however clever. Since the design of machines is one of these intellectual activities, an ultraintelligent machine could design even better machines; there would then unquestionably be an 'intelligence explosion,' and the intelligence of man would be left far behind. Thus the first ultraintelligent machine is the last invention that man need ever make."

The word *singularity* is borrowed from astrophysics: it refers to a point in space-time—for example, inside a black hole—at which the rules of ordinary physics do not apply. In the 1980s the science-fiction novelist Vernor Vinge attached it to Good's intelligence explosion scenario. At a NASA symposium in 1993, Vinge announced that "within 30 years, we will have the technological means to create superhuman intelligence. Shortly after, the human era will be ended."

By that time Kurzweil was also thinking about the Singularity. He'd been busy since his appearance on *I've Got a Secret.* He'd made several fortunes as an engineer and inventor; he'd founded and then sold his first software company while he was still at MIT. He went on to build the first print-to-speech reading machine for the blind—Stevie Wonder was customer No. 1—and made innovations in a range of technical fields, including music synthesizers and speech recognition. (He holds 54 patents and 19 honorary doctorates. In 1999 President Bill Clinton awarded him the National Medal of Technology.)

But Kurzweil was also pursuing a parallel career as a futurist; he has been publishing his thoughts about the future of humankind and machinekind for 20 years, most recently in *The Singularity Is Near,* which was a bestseller when it came out in 2005. A documentary by the same name starring Kurzweil, Tony Robbins and Alan Dershowitz, among others, was released in January 2011. (Kurzweil is actually the subject of two recent documentaries. The other, less authorized but more informative, is called *The Transcendent Man.*) Bill Gates has called him "the best person I know at predicting the future of artificial intelligence."

In real life, the transcendent man is an unimposing

figure who could pass for Woody Allen's even nerdier younger brother. Kurzweil grew up in Queens, N.Y., and you can still hear a trace of it in his voice. Now 65, he speaks with the soft, almost hypnotic calm of someone who gives 60 public lectures a year. As the Singularity's most visible champion, he has heard all the questions and faced down the incredulity many, many times. He's good-natured about it, his manner almost apologetic: *I wish I could bring you less exciting news of the future, but I've looked at the numbers, and this is what they say, so what else can I tell you?*

Kurzweil's interest in humanity's cyborganic destiny began in about 1980, largely as a practical matter. He needed ways to measure and track the pace of technological progress. Even great inventions can fail if they arrive before their time, and he wanted to make sure that when he released his, the timing was right. "Even at that time, technology was moving quickly enough that the world was going to be different by the time you finished a project," he says. "So it's like skeet shooting—you can't shoot at the target." He knew about Moore's law, of course, which states that the number of transistors you can put on a microchip doubles roughly every two years. It's a surprisingly reliable rule of thumb. Kurzweil tried plotting a slightly different curve: the change over time in the amount of computing power, measured in MIPS (millions of instructions per second), that you can buy for $1,000.

As it turned out, Kurzweil's numbers looked a lot like Moore's: they doubled every couple of years. Drawn as graphs, both made exponential curves, with their value increasing by multiples of two instead of by regular increments in a straight line. The curves held eerily steady, even when Kurzweil extended his backward through the decades of pretransistor computing technologies like relays and vacuum tubes, all the way back to 1900.

Kurzweil then ran the numbers on a whole bunch of other key technological indexes—the falling cost of manufacturing transistors, the rising clock speed of microprocessors, the plummeting price of dynamic RAM. He looked even further afield at trends in biotech and beyond—the falling cost of sequencing DNA and of wireless data service and the rising numbers of Internet hosts and nanotechnology patents. He kept finding the same thing: exponentially accelerating progress. "It's really amazing how smooth these trajectories are," he says, "through thick and thin, war and peace, boom times and recessions." Kurzweil calls it the law of accelerating returns: technological progress happens exponentially, not linearly.

## ① The accelerating pace of change …

| Agricultural Revolution | ⟵ 8,000 years ⟶ | Industrial Revolution | ⟵ 120 years |

## ② … and exponential growth in computing power …

Computer technology, shown here climbing dramatically by powers of 10, is now progressing more each hour than it did in its entire first 90 years

**COMPUTER RANKINGS**
By calculations per second per $1,000

**Analytical engine**
Never fully built, Charles Babbage's invention was designed to solve computational and logical problems

**Colossus**
The electronic computer, with 1,500 vacuum tubes, helped the British crack German codes during WW II

BINAC
ENIAC
IBM SSEC
Zuse 3
Zuse 2
IBM Tabulator
National Ellis 3000
Hollerith Tabulator

⟵ ELECTROMECHANICAL ⟶ ⟵ RELAYS ⟶ VACUUM

**1900**          **1920**          **1940**

Then he extended the curves into the future, and the growth they predicted was so phenomenal it created cognitive resistance in his mind. Exponential curves start slowly, then rocket skyward toward infinity. According to Kurzweil, we're not evolved to think in terms of exponential growth. "It's not intuitive. Our built-in predictors are linear. When we're trying to avoid an animal, we pick the linear prediction of where it's going to be in 20 seconds and what to do about it. That is actually hardwired in our brains."

Here's what the exponential curves told him. We will successfully reverse-engineer the human brain

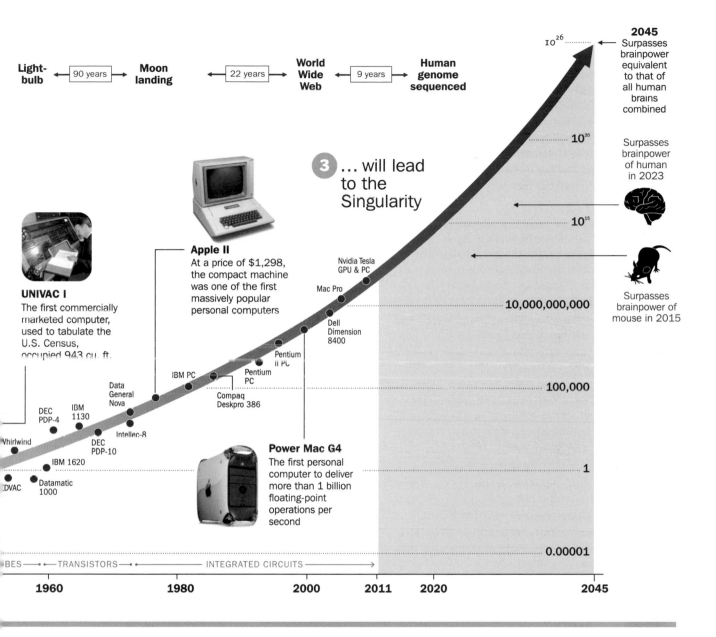

**Light-bulb** ←[ 90 years ]→ **Moon landing** ←[ 22 years ]→ **World Wide Web** ←[ 9 years ]→ **Human genome sequenced**

**2045**
Surpasses brainpower equivalent to that of all human brains combined

$10^{26}$

$10^{20}$

Surpasses brainpower of human in 2023

$10^{15}$

Surpasses brainpower of mouse in 2015

3 ... will lead to the Singularity

**UNIVAC I**
The first commercially marketed computer, used to tabulate the U.S. Census, occupied 943 cu. ft.

**Apple II**
At a price of $1,298, the compact machine was one of the first massively popular personal computers

Nvidia Tesla GPU & PC

Mac Pro

Dell Dimension 8400

10,000,000,000

Pentium II PC

IBM PC

Pentium PC

Data General Nova

Compaq Deskpro 386

100,000

DEC PDP-4

IBM 1130

Intellec-8

DEC PDP-10

Whirlwind

IBM 1620

1

**Power Mac G4**
The first personal computer to deliver more than 1 billion floating-point operations per second

EDVAC

Datamatic 1000

0.00001

BES → ← TRANSISTORS → ← INTEGRATED CIRCUITS →

1960    1980    2000    2011  2020    2045

---

by the mid-2020s. By the end of that decade, computers will be capable of human-level intelligence. Kurzweil puts the date of the Singularity—never say he's not conservative—at 2045. In that year, he estimates, given the vast increases in computing power and the vast reductions in the cost of same, the quantity of artificial intelligence created will be about a billion times the sum of all the human intelligence that exists today.

The Singularity isn't just an idea. It attracts people, and those people feel a bond with one another. Together they form a movement, a subculture; Kurzweil calls it a community. Once you decide to take the Singularity seriously, you will become part of a small but intense and globally distributed hive of like-minded thinkers known as Singularitarians.

Not all of them are Kurzweilians, not by a long shot. There's room inside Singularitarianism for considerable diversity of opinion about what the Singularity means and when and how it will or won't happen. But Singularitarians share a worldview. They think in terms of deep time, they believe in the power of technology to shape history, they have little interest in the conventional wisdom about anything, and they cannot believe you're walking around living your life and watching TV as if the artificial-intelligence revolution were not about to erupt and change absolutely everything. They have no fear of sounding ridiculous; your ordinary citizen's distaste for apparently absurd ideas is just an example of irrational bias, and Singularitarians have no truck with irrationality. When you enter their mind space, you pass through an extreme gradient in worldview, a hard ontological shear that separates Singularitarians from the common run of humanity. Expect turbulence.

In addition to the Singularity University, which Kurzweil cofounded, there's also a Singularity Institute for Artificial Intelligence, based in San Francisco. It counts among its advisers Peter Thiel, a former CEO of PayPal and an early investor in Facebook. The institute holds an annual conference called the Singularity Summit. (Kurzweil cofounded that, too.) Because of the highly interdisciplinary nature of Singularity theory, it attracts a diverse crowd. Artificial intelligence is the main event, but the sessions also cover the galloping progress of, among other fields, genetics and nanotechnology.

At a recent summit, there were not just computer scientists but also psychologists, neuroscientists, nanotechnologists, molecular biologists, a specialist in wearable computers, a professor of emergency medicine, an expert on cognition in gray parrots, and the professional magician and debunker James "the Amazing" Randi. The atmosphere was a curious blend of Davos and UFO convention. Proponents of seasteading—the practice, so far mostly theoretical, of establishing politically autonomous floating communities in international waters—handed out pamphlets. An android chatted with visitors in one corner.

After artificial intelligence, the most-talked-about topic at the summit was life extension. Biological boundaries that most people think of as permanent and inevitable Singularitarians see as merely intractable but solvable problems. Death is one of them. Old age is an illness like any other, and what do you do with illnesses? You cure them. Like a lot of Singularitarian ideas, it sounds funny at first, but the closer you get to it, the less funny it seems. It's not just wishful thinking; there's actual science going on here.

For example, it's well known that one cause of the physical degeneration associated with aging involves telomeres, which are segments of DNA found at the ends of chromosomes. Every time a cell divides, its telomeres get shorter, and once a cell runs out of telomeres, it can't reproduce anymore, and it dies. But there's an enzyme called telomerase that reverses this process; it's one of the reasons cancer cells live so long. So why not treat regular noncancerous cells with telomerase? In November 2010, researchers at Harvard Medical School announced in *Nature* that they had done just that. They administered telomerase to a group of mice suffering from age-related degeneration. The damage went away. The mice didn't just get better; they got younger.

Aubrey de Grey is one of the world's best-known life-extension researchers and a Singularity Summit veteran. A British biologist with a doctorate from Cambridge and a famously formidable beard, de Grey runs a foundation called SENS, or Strategies for Engineered Negligible Senescence. He views aging as a process of accumulating damage, which he has divided into seven categories, each of which he hopes to one day address using regenerative medicine. "People have begun to realize that the view of aging being something immutable—rather like the heat death of the universe—is simply ridiculous," he says. "It's just childish. The human body is a machine that has a bunch of functions, and it accumulates various types of damage as a side effect of the normal function of the machine. Therefore, in principle that damage can be repaired periodically. This is why we have vintage cars. It's really just a matter of paying attention. The whole of medicine consists of messing about with what looks pretty inevitable until you figure out how to make it not inevitable."

Kurzweil also takes life extension seriously. His father, with whom he was very close, died of heart disease at 58. Kurzweil inherited his father's genetic predisposition; he developed Type 2 diabetes when he was 35. Working with Terry Grossman, a doctor who specializes in longevity medicine, Kurzweil has published two books on his own approach to life extension, which involves taking up to 200 pills and supplements a day. He says his diabetes is essentially cured, and although he's 65 years old from a chronological perspective, he estimates that his biological age is about 20 years younger.

But his goal differs slightly from de Grey's. For Kurzweil, it's not so much about staying healthy as long as possible; it's about staying alive until the Singularity. It's an attempted handoff. Once hyperintelligent artificial intelligences

**THE FLOW** *English biologist Aubrey de Grey during a Humanity Plus conference at Caltech. De Grey sees aging as damage that can be repaired.*

arise, armed with advanced nanotechnology, they'll really be able to wrestle with the vastly complex systemic problems associated with aging in humans. Alternatively, by then we'll be able to transfer our minds to sturdier vessels such as computers and robots. He and many other Singularitarians take seriously the proposition that many people who are alive today will wind up being functionally immortal.

It's an idea that's radical and ancient at the same time. In the poem "Sailing to Byzantium," W.B. Yeats describes mankind's fleshly predicament as a soul fastened to a dying animal. Why not fasten it to an immortal robot instead? But Kurzweil finds that life extension produces even more resistance in his audiences than his exponential-growth curves. "There are people who can accept computers being more intelligent than people," he says. "But the idea of significant changes to human longevity—that seems to be particularly controversial. People invested a lot of personal effort into certain philosophies dealing with the issue of life and death. I mean, that's the major reason we have religion."

OF COURSE, A LOT OF PEOPLE THINK THE SINGULARity is nonsense—a fantasy, wishful thinking, a Silicon Valley version of the evangelical story of the Rapture, spun by a man who earns his living making outrageous claims and backing them up with pseudoscience. Most serious critics focus on the question of whether a computer can truly become intelligent.

The entire field of artificial intelligence, or AI, is devoted to this question. But AI doesn't currently produce the kind of intelligence we associate with humans or even with talking computers in movies—HAL or C3PO or Data. Actual AIs tend to be able to master only one highly specific domain, like interpreting search queries or playing chess. They operate within an extremely specific frame of reference. They don't make conversation at parties. They're intelligent, but only if you define intelligence in a vanishingly narrow way. The kind of intelligence Kurzweil is talking about, which is called strong AI or artificial general intelligence, doesn't exist yet.

Why not? Obviously we're still waiting on all that exponentially growing computing power to get here. But it's also possible that there are things going on in our brains that can't be duplicated electronically no matter how many MIPS you throw at them. The neurochemical architecture that generates the ephemeral chaos we know as human consciousness may just be too complex and analog to replicate in digital silicon. The biologist Dennis Bray was one of the few voices

of dissent at that Singularity Summit. "Although biological components act in ways that are comparable to those in electronic circuits," he argued in a talk titled "What Cells Can Do That Robots Can't," "they are set apart by the huge number of different states they can adopt. Multiple biochemical processes create chemical modifications of protein molecules, further diversified by association with distinct structures at defined locations of a cell. The resulting combinatorial explosion of states endows living systems with an almost infinite capacity to store information regarding past and present conditions and a unique capacity to prepare for future events." That makes the ones and zeros that computers trade in look pretty crude.

Underlying the practical challenges are a host of philosophical ones. Suppose we did create a computer that talked and acted in a way that was indistinguishable from a human being—in other words, a computer that could pass the Turing test. (Very loosely speaking, such a computer would be able to pass as human in a blind test.) Would that mean that the computer was sentient, the way a human being is? Or would it just be an extremely sophisticated but essentially mechanical automaton without the mysterious spark of consciousness—a machine with no ghost in it? And how would we know?

Even if you grant that the Singularity is plausible, you're still staring at a thicket of unanswerable questions. If I can scan my consciousness into a computer, am I still me? What are the geopolitics and the socioeconomics of the Singularity? Who decides who gets to be immortal? Who draws the line between sentient and nonsentient? And as we approach immortality, omniscience and omnipotence, will our lives still have meaning? By beating death, will we have lost our essential humanity?

Kurzweil admits that there's a fundamental level of risk associated with the Singularity that's impossible to refine away, simply because we don't know what a highly advanced artificial intelligence, finding itself a newly created inhabitant of the planet Earth, would choose to do. It might not feel like competing with us for resources. One of the goals of the Singularity Institute is to make sure not just that artificial intelligence develops but also that it is friendly. You don't have to be a superintelligent cyborg to understand that introducing a superior life-form into your own biosphere is a basic Darwinian error.

If the Singularity is coming, these questions are going to be answered whether we like it or not, and Kurzweil thinks that trying to put off the Singularity by banning technologies is not only impossible but also unethical and probably dangerous. "It would require a totalitarian system to implement such a ban," he says. "It wouldn't work. It would just drive these technologies underground, where the responsible scientists who we're counting on to create the defenses would not have easy access to the tools."

Kurzweil is an almost inhumanly patient and thorough debater. He relishes it. He's tireless in hunting down his critics so that he can respond to them, point by point, carefully and in detail.

Take the question of whether computers can replicate the biochemical complexity of an organic brain. Kurzweil yields no ground there whatsoever. He does not see any fundamental difference between flesh and silicon that would prevent the latter from thinking. He defies biologists to come up with a neurological mechanism that could not be modeled or at least matched in power and flexibility by software running on a computer. He refuses to fall on his knees before the mystery of the human brain. "Generally speaking," he says, "the core of a disagreement I'll have with a critic is, they'll say, 'Oh, Kurzweil is underestimating the complexity of reverse-engineering of the human brain or the complexity of biology.' But I don't believe I'm underestimating the challenge. I think they're underestimating the power of exponential growth."

IF I CAN SCAN MY CONSCIOUSNESS IN A COMPUTER, AM I STILL ME? WILL OUR LIVES STILL HAVE MEANING?

This position doesn't make Kurzweil an outlier, at least among Singularitarians. Plenty of people make more extreme predictions. Since 2005 the neuroscientist Henry Markram has been running an ambitious initiative at the Brain Mind Institute of the École Polytechnique in Lausanne, Switzerland. It's called the Blue Brain project, and it's an attempt to create a neuron-by-neuron simulation of a mammalian brain, using IBM's Blue Gene supercomputer. So far, Markram's team has managed to simulate one neo-cortical column from a rat's brain, which contains about 10,000 neurons. Markram has said that he hopes to have a complete virtual human brain up and running in 10 years. (Even Kurzweil sniffs at this. If it worked, he points out, you'd then have to educate the brain, and who knows how long that would take?)

By definition, the future beyond the Singularity is not knowable by our linear, chemical, animal brains, but Kurzweil is teeming with theories about it. He positively flogs himself to think bigger and bigger; you can see him kicking against the confines of his aging organic hardware. "When people look at the implications of ongoing exponential growth, it gets harder and harder to accept," he says. "So you get people who really accept, yes, things are progressing exponentially, but they fall off the horse at some point because the implications are too fantastic. I've tried to push myself to really look."

In Kurzweil's future, biotechnology and nanotechnology give us the power to manipulate our bodies and the world around us at will, at the molecular level. Progress hyperaccelerates, and every hour brings a century's worth of scientific breakthroughs. We ditch Darwin and take charge of our own evolution. The human genome becomes just so much code to be bug-tested and optimized and, if necessary, rewritten. Indefinite life extension becomes a reality; people die only if they choose to. Death loses its sting once and for all. Kurzweil hopes to bring his dead father back to life.

We can scan our consciousness into computers and enter a virtual existence or swap our bodies for immortal robots and light out for the edges of space as intergalactic godlings. Within a matter of centuries, human intelligence will have reengineered and saturated all the matter in the universe. This, Kurzweil believes, is our destiny as a species.

OR IT ISN'T. WHEN THE BIG QUESTIONS GET ANSWERED, a lot of the action will happen where no one can see it, deep inside the black silicon brains of the computers, which will either bloom bit by bit into conscious minds or just continue in ever more brilliant and powerful iterations of nonsentience.

But as for the minor questions, they're already being decided all around us and in plain sight. The more you read about the Singularity, the more you start to see it peeking out at you coyly from unexpected directions. A few years ago we didn't have a billion humans carrying out their social lives over a single electronic network. Now we have Facebook. A few years ago you didn't see people double-checking what they were saying and where they were going, even as they were saying it and going there, using handheld network-enabled digital prosthetics. Now we have iPhones. Is it an unimaginable step to take the iPhones out of our hands and put them into our skulls?

Already, 100,000 patients with Parkinson's disease have neural implants. Google is experimenting with computers that can drive cars. There are more than 2,000 robots fighting in Afghanistan alongside human troops. Not long ago, a game show once again figured in the history of artificial intelligence, but this time the computer was the guest: an IBM supercomputer nicknamed Watson competed on *Jeopardy!* Watson runs on 90 servers and takes up an entire room, and in one practice match in January 2011, it finished ahead of two former champions, Ken Jennings and Brad Rutter. It got every question it answered right, but much more important, it didn't need help understanding the questions (or, strictly speaking, the answers), which were phrased in plain English. Watson isn't strong AI, but if strong AI happens, it will arrive gradually, bit by bit, and this will have been one of the bits.

A hundred years from now, Kurzweil and de Grey and the others could be the 22nd century's answer to the Founding Fathers—except that unlike the Founding Fathers, they'll still be alive to get credit—or their ideas could look as hilariously retro and dated as Disney's Tomorrowland. Nothing gets old as fast as the future.

But even if they're dead wrong about the future, they're right about the present. They're taking the long view and looking at the big picture. You may reject every specific article of the Singularitarian charter, but you should admire Kurzweil for taking the future seriously. Singularitarianism is grounded in the idea that change is real, that humanity is in charge of its own fate, and that history might not be as simple as one damn thing after another. Kurzweil likes to point out that your average cellphone is about a millionth the size of, a millionth the price of, and a thousand times as powerful as the computer he had at MIT 40 years ago. Flip that forward 40 years, and what does the world look like? If you really want to figure that out, you have to think very, very far outside the box. Or maybe you have to think farther inside it than anyone ever has before.

# GET SMART

BY JOEL STEIN

*Clearly, our intrepid reporter is no genius. Just look at the experts he consulted on how to become one*

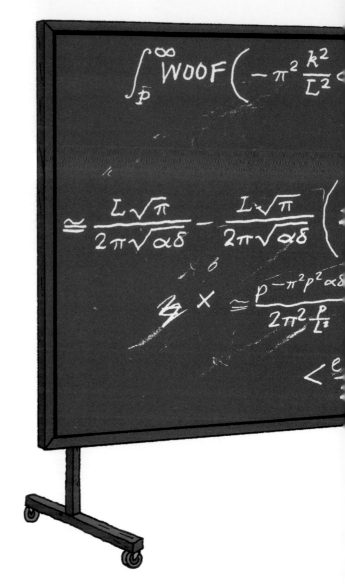

T HOUGH I'VE BEEN CALLED A GENIUS MANY TIMES, IT HAS NEVER BEEN BY ANOTHER PERSON. THIS needed to be rectified. I figured I could probably become more genius-like by studying the lives of geniuses, but is that really how a genius would do it? Wouldn't a genius save time by talking to others who study geniuses? Or better yet, just read an article in a book purchased on a whim in the checkout line? (As you can see, much like Einstein, I like to run *gedankenexperiments*.)

Because that book didn't yet exist, I went with option 1. The first person I tried was Michael Gelb, a motivational speaker and author of books such as *How to Think Like Leonardo da Vinci: Seven Steps to Genius Every Day*; *Innovate Like Edison: The Five-Step System for Breakthrough Business Success*; and the slightly less grandiose *More Balls Than Hands: Juggling Your Way to Success by Learning to Love Your Mistakes*. Gelb said he could tell right away that I had the brain stuff that could be molded into geniusosity because of all the questions I was asking. Until then, I'd humbly thought I asked questions because it's how you do reporting. But no. "The people we call geniuses, like da Vinci, go on asking questions with the same kind of passion and openness that children do," Gelb explained. I considered really impressing him by asking if he liked poop.

Gelb took me through those seven da Vincian principles, none of which seemed particularly life-changing to me. Then he offered his own equally mundane tricks for growing genius, such as keeping a journal, working out, drinking wine and—for businesspeople he gets paid to speak to—smiling like the Mona Lisa. When I asked him to tell me the most genius thing he'd done lately, he said, "I leveraged a trip to New York, getting four days of consulting for a client while my wife got paid to sing for another client. I made a connection most people wouldn't think was possible, and therefore wouldn't think of." He and his wife ate at pricey restaurants and stayed in a great hotel, all at someone else's expense. Comparatively speaking, da Vinci was a moron.

As per Gelb's advice, I increased my wine consumption and notebook doodling, but not one person called

me a genius. In fact, on blogs and Twitter many were calling me much worse. So I contacted Brian Hare, a professor of evolutionary anthropology at Duke and author of *The Genius of Dogs: How Dogs Are Smarter Than You Think*, which he co-wrote with his wife. I'm guessing he's figured out how to expense all sorts of trips—and not just with his wife, but with his dogs, too.

I could learn a lot from dogs, Hare explained, because they are geniuses. I found this hard to believe, given the drooling, leg humping, squirrel chasing, pointless barking, and every single other thing dogs do. Hare argued that although dogs may not learn from their own errors or be able to figure out that when you let go of something, it always drops, they're amazingly skilled at watching humans and other animals solve problems and then copying them. Hare seems to set a pretty low bar for genius.

But then he pointed out that while wolves have been hunted and trapped to a third of their population, dogs have exploded as a species by sucking up to those who can feed and house them. This made me

realize that maybe I am a genius because I don't have a dog. His weak retort was that dogs provide owners with an increase in neuropeptides, oxytocin and other words that don't mean "money" or "sex."

He also tried to argue that walking a dog would get me to meet people outside my social circle, thereby exposing me to new ideas. Though that did seem appealing, I'd argue that talking to anthropology professors exposes me to even more new ideas, and periodic butt sniffing isn't even part of the bargain. When Hare noted that politicians and panhandlers do better when they approach others with dogs in tow, it only made me wish that instead of not having one dog, I could not have two.

By studying dogs—not to mention bonobos—Hare has seen that evolution doesn't even favor intelligence. "It's survival of the friendliest," he said. Evolution has made us kinder. "Animals are self-selecting to be less aggressive and more social. Tigers aren't social at all. Change some genes to make them gregarious, and you wind up with an animal that hunts in groups.

You can become a genius by being more tolerant and friendly." Thomas Edison and Henry Ford weren't lovable, but they were charismatic. If I were nicer, Hare suggested, our conversation would have gone better for me. "You'd have gotten a free book," he said. "And you could have sold it on eBay and made $15." Turns out, people aren't so desperate for $15 if they haven't wasted their money on dog food.

So when I contacted Grady West, who received one of the five Genius Awards given out by Seattle's alternative weekly *The Stranger* last year, I tried being friendlier. And it worked. Maybe too well. West, a drag queen who, as Dina Martina, drinks warm Sprite and doesn't seem to know how to apply lipstick or shave his back, told me his epiphanies come first thing in the morning. "Yesterday I had two revelations," he said. "The first was that Winston Churchill looked like an elderly baby, and the other was that sex offenders make wonderful personal shoppers." Looks like one way to be a genius is to move to Seattle, where the competition is apparently Bill Gates and no one else.

Looking for a more traditional mentor, I tried Odest Jenkins, one of *Popular Science*'s Brilliant 10. Jenkins, an associate professor of computer science at Brown who studies robotics, gave me lots of great advice. Genius, he said, was largely dependent on passion. "If I'm working on projects I'm not that interested in, I'm much less of a genius," Jenkins said. I feel the same way; just look at the questions I asked the dog guy. Jenkins is at his best when he's around other robot lovers—at a conference, the Silicon Valley incubator he's working at while on sabbatical or, I'm guessing, the Battlestar Galactica booth at Comic-Con.

One thing I know I am not interested in is anyone who is really into robots, so I got off the phone. Instead I decided to spend more time with great authors. Even if it didn't make me geniusier, namedropping elite writers would make other writers jealous. And isn't that the true purpose of genius?

George Saunders, the novelist and short-story writer who received a MacArthur genius grant in 2006, said he wanted to answer my questions over e-mail to have more time to compose thoughtful answers. His request gave me my first tip on genius: Don't waste time talking to guys asking stupid questions. His e-mail arrived the next day, giving me my second tip: Don't waste time writing to guys asking stupid questions.

Saunders wrote, "I think the main mark of what we call genius is spontaneous honesty: the ability to say what actually seems true to you in the moment, without a bunch of frills or embellishments. Or to put it another way, geniuses tend to blurt out the big obvious truths that the rest of us have been conditioned to soften, avoid or obfuscate." Mix that kind of honesty with joy, and you have what he calls "saintly insanity," which is a pretty geniusy way of putting it. He listed Hank Williams and Woody Guthrie as artists who expressed thoughts simply and honestly without worrying about being attached to their ideas. Geniuses, I was understanding, are antipoliticians. Also, they need to listen to some new music.

But the best news from Saunders was that I could be more geniusy just by doing more of what I already do: in my case, saying obnoxious stuff. History backs him up. Martin Luther told off the pope; Shakespeare gave it to the Jews; Beethoven took his dead brother's wife's son away from her by calling her slutty; Bobby Fischer gave it to the Jews *even though he was one*; Picasso got women to take off their clothes, then made their breasts look awful; Walt Disney gave it to the Jews *despite the fact that he worked in Hollywood*; Steve Jobs acted like Steve Jobs. I couldn't wait to give it to the Jews. Specifically, my family.

But Saunders, being a genius, predicted my reaction. And so he wrote, in a second paragraph that admittedly I didn't read at first—probably because I got distracted by a Facebook message, then forgot to click back to his e-mail–that simulating the natural, unfiltered genius he was talking about doesn't work. "That attempt might result in what we call the 'a--hole genius'—the guy who always is going around saying what he thinks, no matter what. Actually, that would be just: 'a--hole.'" Unlike genius, that is definitely something I've been called by other people.

And then I realized where Saunders was heading with this concept of genius as pure, natural, joyful honesty. Dogs. Friendly, in-the-moment, subtext-free dogs. They aren't thinking as they hump your leg, *Man, I wish there were an attractive dog around here instead of this scratchy, denim-covered leg. I'm going to be really embarrassed about this in a couple of minutes.* No, they just hump the leg. And then that leg, despite being totally grossed out, takes the dog for a walk so it can clean up after it. Dogs might not get MacArthur genius grants that pay $500,000 over five years, but you don't need that kind of money when someone is paying your rent, buying your food and taking responsibility for all those sanitation tickets.

So I'm going to dog it up. I will befriend the strong and ambitious and watch what they do. And if I see a nice pair of legs, god help them!

# ARE YOU A GENIUS?

*Okay, so you are, in fact, smarter than a fifth-grader. You should be shooting higher. This quiz can tell you if your brain may be big enough for Mensa, the high-IQ society.*

**1.** What is the four-digit number in which the first digit is one-fifth the last, and the second and third digits are the last digit multiplied by 3? (Hint: The sum of all digits is 12.)

**2.** Jane went to visit Jill. Jill is Jane's only husband's mother-in-law's only husband's only daughter's only daughter. What relation is Jill to Jane?

**3.** Which of the words below is least like the others? (The difference has nothing to do with vowels, consonants or syllables.)

MORE, PAIRS, ETCHERS, ZIPPER

**4.** Tabitha likes cookies but not cake. She likes mutton but not lamb, and she likes okra but not squash. Following the same rule, will she like cherries or pears?

**5.** What is the number that is one more than one-tenth of one-fifth of one-half of 4,000?

**6.** In a footrace, Jerry was neither first nor last. Janet beat Jerry, Jerry beat Pat. Charlie was neither first nor last. Charlie beat Rachel. Pat beat Charlie. Who came in last?

**7.** Find the number that best completes the following sequence.

1 2 4 7 11 ? 22

**8.** Marian bought 4 oranges and 3 lemons for 90 cents. The next day she bought 3 oranges and 4 lemons for 85 cents. How much did each lemon and orange cost?

**9.** Start with the number of total mittens the numbered kittens lost, and multiply by the voting age in the U.S. What's the answer?

**10.** There is at least one nine-letter word that contains only one vowel. Do you know what it is?

ANSWERS:

(1) 1,155; (2) Jane's daughter (Jane's mother's husband is Jane's father, his daughter is Jane, and Jill is her daughter.); (3) Zipper (The others can be anagrammed into the names of cities: Rome, Paris, Chester); (4) Cherries (Tabitha only likes food with two syllables.); (5) 41, (4,000 / 2 = 2,000, / 5 = 400, / 10 = 40, + 1 = 41); (6) Rachel; (7) 16 (Each number adds 1, 2, 3, 4, 5 and 6, respectively, to the preceding number); (8) Oranges cost 15 cents each; lemons cost 10 cents each; (9) 216, (3 kittens @ 4 mittens each = 12 x 18, kittens have 4 paws.); (10) Strengths.

**SCORING:** Count the number of correct answers
**9-10** Mensa material! Give them a call.
**7-8** Good chance you're in. But it couldn't hurt to include a cake with your application.
**5-6** Not bad. A little more cramming could put you over the hump.
**BELOW 5** You must have had a bad day.

For more mind-taxing puzzlers, go to www.us.mensa.org/games.

© Dr. Abbie F. Salny

# ABOUT THE AUTHORS

**GARY BELSKY** is the former editor in chief of *ESPN the Magazine*, a columnist for TIME.com and coauthor of the bestseller *Why Smart People Make Big Money Mistakes—and How to Correct Them*.

**DAVID BJERKLIE** is a science writer and the author of children's books on butterflies, agriculture and environmental justice. Formerly, he was the senior science reporter at TIME, senior editor at TIME for Kids, and a science writer and editor at TheVisualMD.com.

**JOHN CLOUD** is a former staff writer for TIME who wrote dozens of features, including cover stories on organic food, gay teenagers, and such diverse figures as Ann Coulter and Howard Dean.

**GEOFF COLVIN**, *Fortune*'s senior editor at large, writes its popular "Value Driven" column. He lectures widely, is the lead moderator for the Fortune Global Forum, and offers daily business commentary on the CBS Radio Network.

**SEAN GREGORY** is a senior writer at TIME, covering sports. He has written profiles of such major figures as LeBron James, Peyton Manning and Roger Goodell.

**LEV GROSSMAN** is TIME's book critic and lead technology writer. He is also the author of two bestselling novels, *The Magicians* and *The Magician King*.

**JEFFREY KLUGER** is a senior editor at TIME, overseeing its science and technology reporting. He has written or co-written more than 40 cover stories for the magazine and regularly contributes articles and commentary on science, behavior and health.

**KELLY KNAUER** has written and edited volumes on Gettysburg, Hurricane Katrina, Planet Earth, Abraham Lincoln and many other subjects for TIME Books. His most recent is *The 100 Most Influential People Who Never Lived*.

**MICHAEL LEMONICK** is a senior science writer at the research organization Climate Central. He covered science for TIME for more than 20 years and is the author of several books on astrophysics.

**BELINDA LUSCOMBE** is an award-winning journalist at TIME. As chief interviewer for its 10 Questions page, she talks to a different newsmaker each week.

**HARRY McCRACKEN** is an editor at large for TIME whose primary beat is technology. He has also edited an animation fanzine, reviewed horror movies and contributed to *The 100 Greatest Looney Tunes Cartoons*.

**MICHAEL NEILL**, who began his journalistic career at the *New York Daily News*, spent 20 years as a writer at *People*, TIME's sister publication.

**REGINA NUZZO** has a doctorate in biostatistics and writes about science and health for *Reader's Digest, Nature News* and other publications.

**JAMES PONIEWOZIK** is the TV and media critic for TIME and writes for the magazine's Tuned In blog.

**ELLEN SHAPIRO** writes and reports for TIME Books and reviews books for *People* magazine.

**JOEL STEIN** is a columnist for TIME. His book, *Man Made: A Stupid Quest for Masculinity*, is in bookstores now.

**MAIA SZALAVITZ**, a writer for TIME.com who specializes in neuroscience, coauthored *Born for Love: Why Empathy Is Essential—and Endangered*.

# PHOTO CREDITS

**FRONT COVER** *(top to bottom)* Popperfoto/Getty Images; David Paul Morris/Getty Images; Corbis; Patrick Kovarik/AFP/Getty Images **BACK COVER** *(left to right, top to bottom)* Bridgeman Art Library/Getty Images; *Portrait of Leonardo da Vinci by Lattanzio Querena, Museo D'Arte Medievale e Moderna, Padova. Photo by DeAgostini/Getty Images;* Culver Pictures/The Art Archive at Art Resource, NY; *Self-Portrait by Vincent Van Gogh, 1889, oil on canvas, Musee d'Orsay, Paris. Photo by Erich Lessing/Art Resource, NY; Wolfgang Amadeus Mozart by Joseph-Siffred Duplessis. Photo by G. Dagli Orti/De Agostini/Getty Images;* Encyclopaedia Britannica/UIG Via Getty Images; Jason Merritt/Getty Images; Comedy Central/Photofest; Mike Ehrmann/Getty Images; Daniel Acker/Bloomberg via Getty Images; Marc Bryan-Brown/Wireimage/Getty Images; Mark Humphrey/AP Images; John M. Burgess/Sports Illustrated; Gedalia Vera/St. Jude; Michael Rougier/Time Life Pictures/Getty Images **FRONT MATTER 1** Photographer unknown **3** Benjamin Bay/The iSpot **6** Ken Orvidas/The iSpot
**THE NATURE OF GENIUS 8** *(left to right)* Bridgeman Art Library/Getty Images; Popperfoto/Getty Images; Jonathan Sprague/Redux; *Self-Portrait by Vincent Van Gogh, 1889, oil on canvas, Musee d'Orsay, Paris. Photo by Erich Lessing/Art Resource, NY;* Corbis **11**. Richard Downs/The iSpot **12** Jonathan Sprague/Redux **13** Dan Burn-Forti/Contour by Getty Images **14** Culver Pictures/The Art Archive at Art Resource, NY **15** *(top)* Bridgeman Art Library/Getty Images **16** *(left)* Adoc Photos/Corbis; *Archimedes by Domenico Fetti, 1589, oil on canvas. Photo by Hans-Peter Klut. BPK, Berlin/Art Resource, NY* **17** The Granger Collection, NY **18** *(left) Portrait of Leonardo da Vinci by Lattanzio Querena, Museo d'Arte Medievale e Moderna, Padova. Photo by DeAgostini/Getty Images;* Corbis **19** *(left)* Grant Delin/Corbis Outline; *School of Athens (Detail of central section with Plato and Aristotle) by Raphael, Stanza della Segnatura, Stanze di Raffaello, Vatican Palace. Photo by Scala/Art Resource, NY* **20** *(left)* Popperfoto/Getty Images; *Wolfgang Amadeus Mozart by Joseph-Siffred Duplessis. Photo by G. Dagli Orti/De Agostini/Getty Images* **21** Mosaic Images/Corbis **23** *Self-Portrait by Vincent Van Gogh, 1889, oil on canvas, Musee d'Orsay, Paris. Photo by Erich Lessing/Art Resource, NY* **24** Mark Asnin/Redux **25** Debra Hurford Brown/Camera Press/Redux **26** Alfred Eisenstaedt/Time Life Pictures/Getty Images
**GENIUS AT WORK**
**28** *(left to right)* Daniel Acker/Bloomberg via Getty Images; Jason Merritt/Getty Images; Comedy Central/Photofest; Mike Ehrmann/Getty Images; Encyclopedia Britannica/UIG via Getty Images **31** Charles Rex Arbogast/AP Images **32** Shelley Gazin/Corbis **33** Everett Collection **34** Bettmann Corbis **35** Science Source **36** *(top)* David Paul Morris/Getty Images; David Yellen/Corbis Outline **37** Robyn Twomey/Corbis Outline **39** Bettmann Corbis **40** Sovfoto/UIG via Getty Images **41** Bettmann Corbis **42** Wally McNamee/Corbis **43** Ira Wyman/Sygma/Corbis **45** Inez and Vinoodh/Trunk Archive **46** Comedy Central/Photofest **47** *(left)* Todd Heisler/The New York Times/Redux Pictures; Richard Ellis/Getty Images **48** Fred Prouser/Reuters/Corbis **49** *(clockwise from top left)* Ian White/Corbis Outline; Isaac Brekken/AP Images; Kevin Mazur/Wireimage for NPG Records/Getty Images **51** *(clockwise from top left)* Timothy Greenfield-Sanders/Corbis Outline; Valerio Mezzanotti/The New York Times/Redux; Rann Chandric/Eyevine/Redux; J. Countess/Getty Images; Miller Mobley/Redux **52** George Pimentel/Getty Images **53** *(left)* Rich Schultz/Getty Images; Art Streiber/©2013 A&E Networks **54** *(clockwise from top left)* BREUEL-BILD/ABB/DPA/Corbis; Rob Kim/Getty Images; Tim P. Whitby/Getty Images **55** Karwai Tang/FilmMagic/Getty Images **56** Jason Schmidt/Trunk Archive **58** Ben Baker/Redux **59** Ralf-Finn Hestoft/Corbis **60** *(top)* Matt Jelonek/Wireimage/Getty Images; George Burns/Harpo Productions via Getty Images **61** John Keatley/Redux **62** Jesse D. Garrabrant/NBAE via Getty Images **64** *(top to bottom)* Jonathan Daniel/Getty Images; Valerio Pennicino/Getty Images; Clive Brunskill/Getty Images **65** Courtesy of Neurocore **66** Mike Ehrmann/Getty Images **67** *(top to bottom)* Mike Ehrmann/Getty Images; Rick Yeatts/Getty Images; Al Bello/Getty Images **68** Gianni Dagli Orti/Corbis **69** Currier & Ives/Library of Congress Prints and Photographs Division **70** *The Spring Mural* (Jackson reviewing his troops in the Shenandoah Valley) from *Four Seasons of the Confederacy: Murals by Charles Hoffbauer/Courtesy of Virginia Historical Society **71** *(top)* Vietnam News Agency/AP Images; Charles Dharapak/AP Images **72** Todd Plitt/Contour by Getty Images **74** A. Barrington Brown/Science Source **75** Brian van der Brug/Pool/Getty Images **76** Underwood & Underwood/Corbis **77** Everett Collection **78** Philip Jones Griffiths/Magnum Photos **79** Christopher Morris/VII/Corbis

**GENIUS AMONG US**
**80** *(left to right)* Marc Bryan-Brown/WireImage/Getty Images; Mark Humphrey/AP Images; John M. Burgess/Sports Illustrated; Gedalia Vera/St. Jude; Photo-illustration by Ryan Schude for TIME **82** Michele Sibiloni/AFP/Getty Images **84** *(top)* Courtesy of The Korea Herald; Margaret Norton/NBC/NBCU Photo Bank via Getty Images **85** Photographer unknown/Courtesy of www.fugue.us **86** Jon M. Fletcher/The Florida Times-Union **87** *(top)* Gedalia Vera/St. Jude; Michael Rougier/Time Life Pictures/Getty Images **88** Jeffrey Coolidge/Getty Images **89** *(top to bottom)* Tom Grill/Getty Images; Clouds Hill Imaging/Corbis; Dorling Kindersley/Getty Images **90** *(clockwise from top left)* Pete Saloutos/Getty Images; Bryan Mullennix/Getty Images; Glow Images/Alamy **91** *(top to bottom)* Jamie Grill/Getty Images; DNY59/E+/Getty Images; Burazin/Getty Images **95** Massimo Merlini/Getty Images **96** *(top) Benjamin Franklin by Joseph Siffred Duplessis, c. 1785, gift of the Morris and Gwendolyn Cafritz Foundation, National Portrait Gallery, Smithsonian Institution—Art Resource, NY;* Tamas Kovacs/EPA/Corbis **97** *(top)* John M. Burgess/Sports Illustrated; Douglas Healey/AP Images **99** Photo-illustration by Phillip Toledano for TIME, prop styling by Donnie Myers **100** Photo-illustration by Ryan Schude for TIME **102** *(left to right)* SSP/Getty Images; SSP/Getty Images; Orlando/Three Lions/Getty Images **103** *(left)* SSP/Getty Images; Apple Computers Inc. **105** Ryan Schude for TIME **109** Illustration by Peter Arkle for TIME **111** Dennis Wunsch/The iSpot